Praise from Cardinals, Bishops, and Laypeople

"*Real People, Real Presence* is a testament to the Lord's power in our daily lives. In this Year of the Eucharist proclaimed by the late Pope John Paul II, *Real People, Real Presence* collects dozens of reflections on the Eucharist, which are invaluable reading for our Eucharistic spirituality. For they invite us into the personal experiences of our brothers and sisters in Jesus Christ. Here we read words of witness from an ageless diversity of believers, from Saint Thomas Aquinas to the person seated next to us at Sunday Mass. I highly recommend *Real People, Real Presence* for all who wish to draw closer to our Eucharistic Lord."

Cardinal Edward Egan Archbishop of New York

"I am very happy to recommend *Real People, Real Presence.* The Holy Eucharist is not simply an idea to be discussed by theologians but rather the actual gift of Jesus Christ present among us. This book shares how ordinary Catholics experience this sacrament as an encounter with the living Lord Jesus. It is the beauty of how this intimate experience of God's love fills the emptiness of our hearts that will help others (re-)discover the true meaning and centrality of finding Jesus in the Holy Eucharist."

Most Reverend Harry J. Flynn
Archbishop of St. Paul and Minneapolis

"With this attractive and deeply personal book, Cardinal Keeler is showing us what the Eucharist means in the lives of people of faith. I hope many will find in it a means of appreciating anew and living more intensely this sacrificial banquet, this real presence that is at the heart of the Church's life."

Cardinal Francis George, OMI, Archbishop of Chicago

"*Real People, Real Presence* is a collection of profound and inspiring testimonies to the love of Jesus in the Eucharist. The ordinary laypeople who wrote them are not great spiritual writers, but their stores *are* great spiritual writing. Let their shared experiences draw you to the Eucharist and nearer to the Lord."

Bert Ghezzi, author of *The Sign of the Cross.*

"I personally recommend *Real People, Real Presence* to all Catholics interested in reflecting, particularly during Mass and Worship of the Eucharist outside of Mass, on what this central Sacrament means to them. In addition, the final chapter could help us all write our own personal witness, perhaps before the Blessed Sacrament, about what Christ's gift of the Eucharist means to us."

Most Reverend Wilton D. Gregory, Archbishop of Atlanta

"The Eucharist is the Source and Summit of our Catholic faith and practice. This volume of reflections and meditations will be a great help to all who seek a deeper appreciation of the Eucharistic Mystery. Here we find the stories of ordinary Catholics who strive to make the connection between the grace of the Eucharist and the disciples' call to live a Eucharistic life of holiness, truth, justice, love, and peace."

Cardinal Roger Mahony, Archbishop of Los Angeles

"*Real People, Real Presence* allows us many different glimpses into the intense faith of "ordinary" Catholics in the Holy Eucharist, a gift and mystery no one of us could ever adequately describe. What better way to appreciate the sacramental mystery of Christ's Body and Blood than through prayerful reflections and confessions of faith from the *members* of His Body, the Church!

"The testimonies are simple and direct; like the Holy Eucharist itself, they speak heart-to-heart. Equally practical and compelling are the extras you will find in this book—short quotes from our late Holy Father and other spiritual writers throughout the centuries on the

Eucharist as well as questions for reflection and discussion at home or in prayer groups. Finally, the book ends with a challenging invitation: Be a 'living witness' to faith in Christ's presence in the Holy Eucharist by the manner of our daily life!"

Cardinal Adam Maida, Archbishop of Detroit

"*Real People, Real Presence* is a book of wonderful stories about the Lord's Presence through the Eucharist in the lives of some faith-filled people. The stories give you a smile, a sigh, inspiration, and sometimes a tear, but they always have the true sound of reality and the true sense of the Lord's divine, loving Presence in this great sacrament. I commend all those who are part of this very fascinating and worthwhile project for enhancing our deeper understanding of God's goodness in giving us the Eucharist. I recommend it heartily as food for thought, for meditation, and for true growth in holiness."

Cardinal Theodore McCarrick, Archbishop of Washington

"In the Eucharist we find the motivation and strength to work for a more just society and to care for one another. The Eucharist is a sacrament of unity. The more we are united to each other, the more deeply we shall experience the presence and love of Jesus in the Eucharist. Through the prayers and reflections of *Real People, Real Presence* may we more deeply appreciate Christ's gift of Himself to us, and may we make a gift of ourselves to God and to others."

Most Reverend Seán P. O'Malley, OFM Cap
Archbishop of Boston

"I happily recommend this beautiful collection of testimonies by ordinary Catholics who share their personal encounters with Jesus in the Holy Eucharist. These testimonies of Eucharistic faith and love are a positive sign that our beloved Pope John Paul II's hope of rekindling amazement in the Eucharist is being realized. May all who read this book be drawn to a deeper appreciation of the Eucharistic mystery, the source and summit of our Christian life."

Most Reverend Kevin C. Rhoades, Bishop of Harrisburg

"*Real People, Real Presence* is a fitting response to the call and legacy of Pope John Paul II to deepen Eucharistic faith in the Church. The reflections and stories contained here reflect the faith of ordinary people in our Lord truly present in the most holy Eucharist. In *Real People, Real Presence,* we see how that faith has been deepened in the lives of various people with the passing of time, as they have faced difficulties in life and experienced its joys. It is this same Lord Jesus, present in the Eucharist, who has sustained them and helped them to persevere in the Christian life.

"I recommend *Real People, Real Presence* to all the faithful as a means of deepening their own faith in this great mystery of our Lord and Savior Jesus Christ present in the Blessed Sacrament."

Cardinal Justin Rigali, Archbishop of Philadelphia

"All of us lament the hectic pace of everyday life but seem helpless to change it. The stories contained in *Real People, Real Presence* show us the way. If we are willing to put the Lord first in our daily lives, we will soon find more time available than we ever expected. We will begin to experience a peace that has nothing to do with all our responsibilities and everything to do with a generous God. This is a great grace in this Year of the Eucharist!"

Sister Ann Shields, author of *Fire in My Heart*

REAL PEOPLE, REAL PRESENCE

Ordinary Catholics on the Extraordinary Power of the Eucharist

Presented by
CARDINAL WILLIAM H. KEELER

With a Foreword by
Fr. Benedict Groeschel, CFR

the WORD among us® press

The Word Among Us Press
9639 Doctor Perry Road
Ijamsville, Maryland 21754
www.wordamongus.org

ISBN: 1-59325-064-9

Cover design by Evelyn Harris
Text design by David Crosson

Made and printed in the United States of America

Library of Congress Control Number: 2005930242

TABLE OF CONTENTS

FOREWORD

by Fr. Benedict J. Groeschel, CFR

When my friend Cardinal Keeler of Baltimore asked me to write a foreword to this beautiful book on the Holy Eucharist, I was quite pleased. However, when he sent me a selection of the testimonies laypeople wrote about their experiences with the Holy Eucharist, I was delighted and, to some degree, astounded. For years I have been working on the psychology of religious experience and devotion, and I did not expect to find that this selection of people would so clearly demonstrate precisely what religious devotion is.

The first Christian prayer to the ascended Savior is recorded in the seventh chapter of the Acts of the Apostles, with the death of Saint Stephen. As Saint Luke tells us, this young man, about to be stoned to death, was deeply aware of the presence of Christ: "But he, full of the Holy Spirit, gazed into heaven and saw the glory of God, and Jesus standing at the right hand of God; and he said, 'Behold, I see the heavens opened, and the Son of man standing at the right hand of God'" (Acts 7:55-56). In response to this experience of Christ's very real presence, Saint Stephen does two things: he follows Christ's commandment to forgive his enemies, and he trusts in God completely. Thus, devotion includes two elements: a profound awareness and a heartfelt response. One of the greatest Catholic authorities on devotion, Saint Francis de Sales, gives us that analysis of devotion in his classic *Treatise on the Love of God*.

If we look carefully at the experiences related in this book, we see that both elements are to be found in these selections, particularly the first: an awareness of Christ's presence is clearly enunciated. The other step is not always as clearly present, because the writers did not put down their full experience. From several of the writers, and no doubt from discussion with the others, we could realize that they all came away from the experience of Christ's presence with a sense of wanting to do Christ's will and trusting in him amid the difficulties and trials of life.

What a magnificent gift Catholics have in the Eucharist! Not only can we assist at Christ's sacrifice celebrated every day and receive him in Holy Communion daily or frequently, but we also have the marvelous opportunity of being sacramentally in his presence as often as circumstances permit. Devotion to the Real Presence has grown over the centuries, particularly because of the initial influence of Saint Francis of Assisi. In my book *In the Presence of Our Lord* (Our Sunday Visitor, 1997), I outline the history of this devotion to the Eucharistic presence of Christ and what it has come to mean to individuals and to the church.

Those who experience Christ in the Eucharist individually will be eager to pray fervently and often in his presence. Such prayer changes our lives. It opens the soul and makes it more docile to God's inspirations, giving us courage and strength and letting us know that we are never alone. Those deeply aware of the meaning of Christ's presence in the Eucharist have no reason to fear loneliness, because they know that Christ is with us: "Behold, I am with you always, to the close of the age" (Matthew 28:20). These words of our Savior—the last he spoke on earth, as recorded in Saint Matthew's gospel—have stayed with the church through the centuries and have led people to the wonderful experience of the Eucharistic presence.

The friars and sisters of our community, who live and work with the very poor, have often spoken of the unusual experience of elderly African American Protestant women who come and pray before the Blessed Sacrament in our church in the Bronx. Although they are not Catholic, they tell one another, "You go to pray in that church, and the sweet Lord Jesus is there. You could tell because you could feel him there."

It would be wonderful if all Catholics took the time and gave the necessary prayerful attention in order to be aware of Christ's presence in the Eucharist. Like any other presence, it will be real and personal to us to the degree that we respond to it. Response is essential to experience. We can be sitting next to someone on a bus and be completely un-present to them, since we don't know them or care to know them. We do not attend or respond to them. On the other hand, we can talk to someone on the telephone 10,000 miles away, and they may be very truly present to us. Presence requires response, among other things.

This means that Christ is there in the Blessed Sacrament waiting for us, but we will realize this only if we are there watching and waiting for him. The marvelous testimonies in this book, done with simplicity and no previous expectations, illustrate why Catholic devotion to the Eucharist survives all attempts to obliterate it or reduce it to a secondary place in the Christian life. Christ is there in the tabernacle, and those who take the trouble to find him will know that this is true.

Father Benedict J. Groeschel, CFR
St. Crispin Friary
Bronx, New York

INTRODUCTION

by Cardinal William H. Keeler

Archbishop of Baltimore

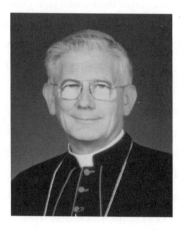

I n October 2004, six months before he died, Pope John Paul II issued an apostolic letter dedicating the entire year— through October 2005—to the Eucharist. To celebrate this Year of the Eucharist, I invited the people of the Archdiocese of Baltimore to submit their personal testimony about their love of Jesus in the Eucharist. Our hope, fulfilled in these pages, was to raise the hearts of people to a renewed appreciation of the Eucharist as God's sacred gift.

The stories and reflections that follow were written by ordinary parishioners, not professionals. They speak simply about their life experiences from a personal perspective: about experiencing Christ in the Eucharist in Sunday or weekday Mass, serving as an extraordinary minister, taking Communion to the sick, or spending time before Jesus in the Blessed Sacrament. Each of these testimonies, coming from people of a variety of ages and situations, offers its own small window into the wonder of the Eucharist and the great possibility that the presence of Christ holds for each of our lives. Every writer of these witnesses answers the question "Do you love the Eucharist?" with a resounding yes!

Taken together, the stories in *Real People, Real Presence* compose a song of love to the Lord, striking a variety of chords and resonating from deep within. We hope that as you read the stories here, this love song will resonate deep within you as well. To add even more to your prayerful reflection, we have included quotes on the Eucharist from Pope John Paul II and from the church's saints, as well as questions for discussion and reflection after each chapter.

I invite you to read these pages gently, allowing the reverence in your own heart to expand. Even further, I propose that you allow these stories to inspire the writing and sharing of your own story. To be profound, your story doesn't require miracles or dramatic circumstances. As long as it is real, then there is power in it—God's power alive in you and in your sharing.

To that end, a brief section has been included in the back of this book with some guidance on how to write and share your own story. Our hope is that the sharing of the testimonies contained in these pages will propel your own witness and the witness of thousands of others. The gift of Jesus in the Eucharist is God's gift to us *and through* us to bless others who might hear it.

May God grant that you increase your desire to fall deeply in love with Jesus Christ through the intimate encounter of the Eucharist. Be inspired yourself by these testimonies, be renewed in your sense of wonder and awe, be surrendered to God's Holy Spirit dwelling deep within your heart. Then be God's witness! No one else can take your place. No one else encounters the exact people you do in the exact circumstances that you do. No calling is greater than this one. And your circumstances need not change for you to exercise it. If any change is needed, it is only your desire to live and love differently within those circumstances.

During his lifetime, Pope John Paul II taught us so very much. His call to reflect on the Eucharist is one of his last gifts to us. Provided in the appendix is the complete text of his apostolic letter for the Year of the Eucharist, which offers the source of inspiration for this movement of the Spirit. In an address delivered in January 2004, the Holy Father asked that bishops, in collaboration with priests, religious, and the faithful, give "the maximum commitment to reflecting on and deepening this essential dimension of the sacramental life of the Church," and work "to awaken an ever greater love for the Mystery of the Eucharist in their dioceses." As the loving awe of Jesus' presence in the Eucharist grows among God's people, may we awaken to the enormous possibilities for our world. And beyond the awe of being in God's presence, imagine what miracles of healing, care, and love God can do today acting through those who actually receive God's presence in the Eucharist. That is our sacred privilege!

At the very beginning of his pontificate, Pope Benedict XVI renewed the call to deepen our love for the Eucharist in this special year:

> My Pontificate begins in a particularly meaningful way as the Church is living the special year dedicated to the Eucharist. How could I fail to see this providential coincidence as an element that must mark the ministry to which I am called? The Eucharist, the heart of Christian life and the source of the Church's evangelizing mission, cannot but constitute the permanent center and source of the Petrine ministry that has been entrusted to me. The Eucharist makes constantly present the Risen Christ who continues to give himself to us, calling us to participate in the banquet of his Body and his Blood. From full communion with him flows every other element of the Church's life: first of all, communion among all the faithful, the commitment to proclaiming and witnessing to the Gospel, the ardor of love for all, especially the poorest and lowliest.

All royalties from the sale of this book will be donated to Catholic education and the restoration of the sacred and historic Basilica of the Assumption of the Blessed Virgin Mary in Baltimore, Maryland. I express my deep gratitude to all who made this work possible. I am grateful to all who shared their testimonies and regret that we could not include more. I thank Patty Mitchell, Margaret Procario, and Jeff Smith of The Word Among Us Press for their counsel, diligence, and support of this worthy endeavor. I also express my sincere gratitude to TJ Sonni, who originated the project idea and helped to shepherd it along the way.

Open your heart greater than ever to God's tidal force of Eucharistic love. Allow yourself to be God's holy and humble instrument to share this wonderful love story with others. May the peace and Eucharistic love of Jesus Christ be with you now and forever!

CHAPTER 1

Gift and Mystery

The Church has received the Eucharist from Christ her Lord not as one gift—however precious— among so many others, but as *the gift par excellence*, for it is the gift of himself, of his person in his sacred humanity, as well as the gift of his saving work.

—Pope John Paul II

A Year Too Soon

by Kevin Wells

My guess is that Holly Martin's and my elocution abilities were mildly advanced, because we were chosen as lectors for a bimonthly school Mass. And because we were willing participants in the celebration of Mass, we were afforded luxury seats at the altar, close to the celebrant, Fr. Charles Brown. None of our seventy-or-so second-grade classmates at St. Pius X had made their first Communion—and neither had Holly and I.

However, that didn't stop Fr. Brown from solemnly walking toward us at Communion time with the host in his fingertips.

That was an oversight.

He stopped directly in front of me, stooped down, and said four words that had never been spoken to me before: "The body of Christ." Not knowing what else to do, I mumbled something, opened my mouth as wide as I could, and received my first Holy Communion—not only a year too soon but while my mom was likely at home washing the dishes. Fifteen minutes later, Mom wasn't doing dishes anymore. She was breaking the speed limit in our yellow and brown station wagon, flying to my Bowie, Maryland, school to meet her son in the principal's office.

I remember thinking with Holly that something odd had just taken place—but we couldn't quite put a finger on it. We knew that we shouldn't have accepted the host, but we figured—immaturely—that it was probably a perk for those fortunate enough to be seated at the altar. Plus, we weren't about to turn down Fr. Brown. No one disobeyed Fr. Brown.

However, after Mass, we were immediately approached by both of the second-grade teachers and rushed down to the office to meet with our principal, Sr. Jane. Parents were called. Fr. Brown was told of his accidental error. Holly and I were surrounded by frowning elders in the tiny principal's office, and rumors started filtering through the hallways.

We were in big trouble. Jesus had come too soon.

It was then—thirty-or-so years ago—that I began to fathom the awesome significance of the real presence of Christ in the Eucharist. My mistake came with a jarring but unforgettably beautiful realization: this precious centerpiece of my Catholic faith—the Eucharist—should never be taken lightly. I realized then—enveloped by anxious adults—that shattering a windowpane with an errant baseball throw, pulling my sister Chrissy's hair, or refusing to empty the trash belonged in an entirely different category from accepting the Eucharist before it was my time. Although I didn't comprehend it then, the basic underpinnings of my devotion to the Holy Eucharist were laid that day.

Now, as a married adult with two children, I can't imagine my life without Jesus Christ at its marrow. How wonderful that our faith has bequeathed so many gifts to us—the sacraments, Scripture groups, retreats, spiritual guidance, outreaches, good friends, schooling, bull and oyster roasts, and the like. But all of it would be rendered virtually meaningless without the marvelous miracle of Christ present in the Eucharist.

When Jesus dined with the twelve the night before his death, he altered the normal course of the typical Passover meal and made himself the focus. He broke some bread, gave it to his friends, and said, "This is my body. It has been given up for you. Do this in memory of me." With those words, he ignited both our mystery and our Catholic faith. Without those words—and the realization that the sacrificial presence of Christ actually is with us each time at Mass (in the same manner as if Jesus walked through the church doors to celebrate alongside us)—our church would not be the same.

The powerful reality of our faith is that our church has never wavered from its belief that Christ shares his love and life with us through the Eucharist. In an unbelievably intimate and loving way, Christ chooses to give himself freely to us regardless of our condition. We can approach Christ at Communion weakened, saddened, fatigued, confused, or—tragically—bored, but because our Savior loves us so much, he chose to give of himself no matter what our condition. And that's the daunting part of the Eucharistic equation: at Communion we can accept the Real Presence without ourselves being "really present." Christ takes that chance with us—he offers himself in this sacred banquet regardless of our condition. As a maturing Catholic, I know I should consider the sacredness of the exchange and receive him only when I feel I'm prepared.

I believe that our faith took root the moment Jesus consecrated the bread and wine in front of the gaping eyes of his twelve friends. And at each Mass, when the celebrant slowly lowers his palms at the consecration, I know I am witnessing something both sacrificial and miraculous. We would not be a unified, thriving church without that powerfully mysterious, blessed sacrifice.

Holly and I were wide-eyed, silly kids. We should have kept our mouths shut. But the fact is, something momentous took root in me that day. Christ became part of me in a radical, giving, real way.

He did for Holly, too.

A Walk of Faith

by Rosanne Deludos

A few years ago I attended the first Communion Mass for my cousin's son at Our Lady of Hope Church in Baltimore. A young lady with physical disabilities was also making her first Communion. I have never been touched so deeply. This young woman decided that she would literally "walk to the table" to receive Christ for the first time. With the help of two adults, she made her way to the altar, where Fr. John Ward was waiting. He was so patient with her as she tried to take Christ in her mouth. It did require a few tries and a few wipes with the cloth. But as she turned to return to her seat, the smile on her face was priceless! I'm sure there wasn't a dry eye in the church.

Every time I make my way through the line to receive Communion, I think of that young lady and how much she was willing to struggle. I haven't since nor will I ever again take for granted the privilege of receiving Christ.

"What a Friend We Have in Jesus"

by Linda K. Langdon

My dear mom passed away on my birthday last year. My sisters and I were with her, singing her favorite hymns, as a tear rolled down her cheek. There's no question—she heard us. She was surrounded by the caretakers who had provided for and loved her over the past four years, as she left our arms and entered the embrace of Jesus.

Mom was a good woman and a Presbyterian who played an integral part in raising us as Catholics. Meatless Fridays were her specialty. Nevertheless, after her passing, I was consumed with anxiety about whether she had "made it" to heaven. On the morning we were to meet with her pastor regarding her funeral plans, I paid my weekly visit to the Eucharist in our adoration chapel. Alone, I shared my grief with the Lord to the point of tears. I trusted him, and I knew in my heart that he loved Mom even more than I did, but my all-too-human doubts kept getting in my way.

At our meeting with her pastor, we shared that Mom's favorite prayers had always been hymns. When we began to name some of them, I blurted out, "What a Friend We Have in Jesus," and her pastor wrote it down. I don't even know why I said it, because it wasn't one of Mom's favorites.

The following day I attended Mass and found myself terribly distracted. In the background, music was playing but no one was singing. All at once the Holy Spirit inspired me to listen to the music. I focused and discovered that the organist was playing "What a Friend We Have in Jesus." A huge smile spread across my face. It was a song I had never heard played in a Catholic service before. My doubts were dispelled, and I knew I had my answer—Mom was in heaven. After Communion, the meditation hymn "Soul of My Savior" was played. That was my dad's favorite. Throughout their lives, theirs was a perfect example of a loving marriage; I believed that God was letting me know that now they were together once again. My mourning was over. What an extraordinary gift to receive in the already extraordinary celebration of the Eucharist.

Later that day I shared my story with our music director, who informed me that nothing she had played that morning had been on the schedule for that Mass. She said that she didn't know why she played the songs she did. Well, I knew why.

Whenever we visit the Lord in the Eucharist, we are always given tremendous blessings. Jesus is a great listener, a consummate consoler, and is tirelessly patient and loving. Sometimes we are even fortunate enough to recognize his blessings. I was blessed to know that Jesus welcomed my mom into his loving embrace. It's quite true what our Protestant friends say: "What a Friend We Have in Jesus"!

The Bell

by TJ Sonni

From my earliest memories, I have always held a profound love and respect for the Eucharist. As a seven-year-old altar boy, I recall mustering my strength to reach up and brace the venerable Msgr. Mann as he stepped down from the altar to give Communion to the people who knelt at the rail. This, of course, was after I got to ring the bell at the appointed times during the consecration. Nearly forty years later, I found myself at a daily Mass as a lector, kneeling to the side of the altar in the sanctuary as the Eucharistic prayer unfolded. Despite the passage of time, the panic reflex struck me when the priest lifted the body of Christ and said the words, "This is my body." I was momentarily stunned by the silence. "The bell!" I suddenly thought. "Did I forget to ring the bell?" Then I breathed a sigh of relief and laughed quietly as I thought to myself, "We don't ring the bell at the consecration anymore, and you're not the altar boy!"

Attending daily Mass has been an extraordinary privilege for me. Over the years, I have fallen in and out of the practice. When I am there, I can hardly imagine why more people don't come to Mass every day. And why don't I? Daily Mass is very different from Sunday Mass. It has a beauty and a power in its quietness, peacefulness, and simplicity.

I've also been blessed with many moments of grace at Mass, especially when serving as a Eucharistic minister. On one particular occasion, I remember experiencing a profound and lasting joy as I offered the body of Christ with love to every person who came to me. The Eucharist is the sacrament of love. When presenting the host, I try to look each person in the eye and yet become transparent myself—allowing them to have a true encounter with Christ, whose love can heal whatever hurt, whatever pain, whatever poverty each person brings to the table of the Lord. It is a deeply transforming experience to reflect God's love for his people, one after another, all shapes and sizes, all ages and circumstances. God loves each one equally and profoundly. I am too weak to do so myself in human terms. But when I serve as a Eucharistic minister, God does it through me if I totally surrender to him.

There is no place else on earth where the richest and poorest can stand together to receive the most precious of gifts—Christ himself. None of us—whatever our circumstances—can ever deserve it, and yet it is offered freely to us out of God's unfathomable love for us all. In the Eucharist, if only for a few moments, I live the body of Christ—one in love with God through his Son, Jesus, and one with my brothers and sisters in that same love. Can I live the sacrament beyond those moments? Can I be a sacrament to others, as the Lord intends? Most of the time I fail. But the Lord never fails to forgive me when I do. In my brokenness and weakness his grace and power shine through even more.

Serving as a greeter welcoming people to Mass recently, I realized that my ministry that day was simply an extension of the Eucharist. As I greeted each person, I silently offered the words, "The body of Christ." Christ in my body. Christ in the body of the community. Just Christ. Could I allow God to live in me at least long enough to love each person equally and give myself to them fully with just a simple greeting or smile or handshake? Something clicked for me that day regarding the call to be the body of Christ for others beyond the church walls. I've heard and known about that call. That day I lived it a little.

Beyond Sunday and daily Masses, I have had numerous experiences of grace and joy before the Blessed Sacrament. The most dramatic have been on retreat weekends when I have made time to get a tiny glimpse of the power and presence of Christ in the Eucharist through adoration of the Blessed Sacrament.

In addition, engaging in a middle-of-the-night Eucharistic adoration every week for seven years offered me regular mini-retreats as well as many graces for which I was largely unready and always undeserving. Even when I could hardly stay awake and sometimes probably didn't, I experienced the grace of God's overcoming love. He doesn't need much from me—just a nanosecond of true attention and a desire to pour forth his love.

Even with all that I have learned and experienced in my life, I feel like I hardly have a clue about the full depth and power and beauty of the Eucharist. But I am trying to be open to God's call. With unceasing patience, the good Lord continues to ring the bell for me: "TJ, pay attention now."

A Gift of Gratitude

by Lori Brooks

We are reminded often that the Eucharist is God's great gift of love to us. What I struggle with is how to express my gratitude. How do I say thank you for this gift of love—for life, for my husband, for my children, for everything God has given me?

I understand how to make simple expressions of thanks

that satisfy my need to show my gratitude for the kindnesses I receive from friends and family. And when I look around me, I see the lovely ways that people express their appreciation to one another. Semester after semester, a young boy uses the pen that was a gift from his teacher. Whenever she visits her grandmother, a teenage girl wears the special locket that her grandmother gave her for her birthday. After she recovers from her surgery, a friend returns a casserole dish, and it is overflowing with cookies. Through such acts of thoughtfulness, the need to express gratitude seems to be satisfied.

When the very word "Eucharist" means "thanksgiving," how do we show our gratitude? I know that each and every day I am presented with a multitude of ways to show my appreciation. But the mystery is deepened when the tiniest prayer of thanks offered seems to be reflected back at me, illuminating an infinite array of other opportunities for thanksgiving. When *our desire to thank God is itself his gift to us,* then life becomes a beautiful, never-ending, life-giving cycle of thanksgiving. Thank you, Father, for your awesome gift to us of Jesus in the Eucharist.

God's Great Gift of Love

by Doris Albrecht

I remember my first Holy Communion quite vividly, even though it happened so many years ago. Oh, what preparation there was! The study of our catechism. The anxiety of going to confession for the very first time, and the relief that followed. The excitement of getting my dress, veil, and shoes. The gift of my first rosary, scapular, and prayer book—all white, of course! It was such a joyful time, filled with so much anticipation.

Finally, at long last, the moment to receive my first Communion arrived. What amazement I felt at that moment to think that the Lord who made me was coming to me in such a special way! To this day, I receive Communion with great anticipation, wonder, and awe at the loving presence of Christ with me. I am filled with joy, love, a thankful heart, and a renewed spirit to face the challenges of a new day. What a profound mystery and sacrament of love! My prayer will always be,

O, Jesus in the Blessed Sacrament,

I love you, I adore you, I praise you, and I thank you. Amen.

A Boy Discovers Peace

by Bill Wingard, Jr.

"William, this is very difficult for me to tell you, but your mother just died this morning, and your father will be by to pick you up. We will be praying for you." The nun who uttered these dreaded words was my first-grade teacher. I left school that day a stunned, saddened, very confused little boy.

About two weeks later I was back at my Catholic grammar

school as usual, but something was wrong, very wrong. I had this feeling of being alone—as if I had been abandoned—and it wouldn't go away. Yes, my father was there. Yes, I knew that he loved me, but a big chunk of me was missing. Class routine helped replace the daydreams that arrived when my mother left, but the real hurt was deeper inside. I wasn't expecting what came next.

Once a month or so our class would gather in the small school chapel for Eucharistic devotion. The gold monstrance that contained the host looked majestic and formidable. It had gold spokes that looked like rays pointing out in all directions. In its center was the very host that the priest held up at Mass. The nuns said this was actually Jesus' body. We were all told to be very quiet and just kneel or sit. This is something that doesn't come naturally to first-graders. Yet somehow we knew that something far bigger than us was present. In that little chapel room an awareness of warmth and happiness came over me, and I sensed that God wanted to tell me something that would get to the real hurt deep inside me. With a voice that was at once awesomely quiet yet very clear, God spoke to me in the solitude of my mind and heart: "I will never abandon you. You are special to me." At once that intense loneliness went away, and in its place was a joy deeper than words could describe. This was the beginning of my life-long love affair with Jesus in the Eucharist.

I was an altar boy during my junior-high and high-school years. These years were filled with turmoil, but God always seemed to keep his promise of looking after me. I still had a feeling of closeness to him, and the reality of his presence in the tabernacle was unavoidable. It seemed that he was waiting for me whenever I went inside a church. That silent, clear voice still spoke reassurance rather than condemnation, even when correcting me for my many sins. I always knew that it was him speaking to me. His voice was never judgmental.

My life's journey after high school led to Maryknoll Seminary. But after a little over a year, I left confused and depressed about what God really wanted from me. I just knew that the priesthood wasn't working. On a deeper level I felt that my life was off the course that God had plotted for me.

Things got worse. My thinking warped, and closeness with God was no longer the driving force in my life. In short, I rebelled. Yet, even in the midst of rebellion, while following others who couldn't care less about a closer walk with God, I would occasionally stumble into a church and wonder. The sense of his presence was still there. Eventually God won out. Even though I had run from him, he never reneged on his promise to look after me. Once again he met me in the lonely darkness of my soul, and the embers of my love for him flickered and then became a flame.

I'm married now, and the Eucharist is the central reality of my life. In St. John's gospel Jesus says that if we eat his flesh and drink his blood we will have life. To me, that's like partaking in the very essence of God. When I receive him, there is a change in my heart, in my emotions, and in every part of my being. Yes, there is a faith component to receiving Jesus in the Eucharist, but both faith and truth work together to form the undeniable experience of his presence, love, and beauty.

My prayer is that more people will take the opportunity

to talk to God—whether in a church or wherever they might find themselves. Jesus is waiting to give us his love and support, and through the Eucharist, to give us his entire being. We can't get any closer than that.

A Daily Miracle

by Hope Heaven Hatch

To me, the Eucharist is a precious gift that God has given me. I feel so blessed. I have this gift to look forward to every day. Like a patient father waiting for his child, God waits for me to come to Mass to share this special time with him! All I have to do is come, and he is there, ready to share himself, body and soul, with me.

During the Mass I enjoy the comfort of being in community, seeing my neighbors and friends together in prayer. It is a joyful time. There is happiness in the songs we sing. The readings and the homily always provide teachings that I hunger for. But the climax of the Mass is still ahead.

As the offertory approaches I begin to concentrate on what is about to happen, and I can't help but thank God for this amazing blessing. As the priest raises the consecrated host and the church is silent as all eyes focus on the altar, Christ is right there with us—body and soul! I wonder how I can be so privileged to be in his very presence. As the priest raises the chalice, I can't help but think how he must feel to witness this same miracle every day. It must be an overwhelming experience!

As I approach the altar, I bow to my Lord and Savior. With my hands folded in prayer, all I can think of is how unworthy I am! As I receive Christ's body and blood and walk back to my pew, I reflect in wonder at the fact that I actually have my precious Jesus in my mouth! I have held him in my hand, felt him on my tongue, tasted his blessed body! When I reach my pew, I kneel silently and hope that these few moments will last forever. At one point, I open my eyes and look toward the altar. There I see Jesus—in his gorgeous white robes, hands outstretched, smiling warmly at me. There are angels all around him! I look into his eyes and feel the comfort only a child in the embrace of a parent feels. Although I know that I am still on earth, the Eucharist brings me so close to Jesus that I feel like I am with him in heaven!

All over the earth, eyes are focused on the altar as the Mass is celebrated throughout the world every day. Catholics every-where—in South America, Russia, Japan—are also receiving this precious gift. The Eucharist brings us together as the body of Christ. It is the most incredible gift we can ever receive on this earth, yet it is only a glimpse into what awaits us in heaven. O precious Jesus, thank you for the gift of the Holy Eucharist. Thank you for giving me your body to strengthen me as I go about my daily work. I look forward to our special time again when I will receive you—body, blood, soul, and divinity—in the Holy Eucharist.

The Answer to My Prayer

by Colleen N. Garrett

My father was one of fifteen children. His parents were devout Catholics—second-generation Germans from Bavaria. My paternal grandparents passed their Catholic faith on to their children, and my father passed that faith on to his children.

My father only had a fourth-grade education. When he was nine years old, he was in a trolley accident that left him deaf in one ear and barely able to hear in the other. He dropped out of school and became an apprentice to a plumber. He was a self-taught, hard-working person who earned his master plumber's degree on his own. Every night we saw him spend hours reading the newspaper from cover to cover.

My father saw to it that his children were brought up in the Catholic faith. He sent all five of us to a parochial school. It would have been easier financially to send us to a public school. It was difficult for him to manage the tuition for a private school on a plumber's salary. But it was important to him to give his children a Catholic education.

Despite my father's devotion to his Catholic faith, I never saw him receive the sacraments. The reason was that his first marriage ended in divorce after he discovered that his wife had been unfaithful. Because of the divorce, he married our mother before a justice of the peace. But he attended Mass every Sunday. He made sure that his children never took a single bite to eat before saying grace. And he made sure that his children were raised as Catholics.

I attended Saints Peter and Paul Catholic School in Cumberland, Maryland, for grades one through eight. Then I attended Ursuline Academy—in the same building—for grades nine through twelve.

The schools were located beside Saints Peter and Paul Catholic Church. The eight o'clock Mass was filled every morning with students from twelve grades! We attended Mass together as a class, and then we walked next door to begin our daily instruction. Every morning at Mass for all those years, right at the consecration of the host, I prayed a special prayer—that my father and mother would be able to receive the sacraments before they died.

In 1967, when I was twenty-four years old, I received a phone call from my dad asking me to please come home for Easter that year. (I was living in Baltimore County at the time.) However, he didn't say why he was so eager for me to come.

My father, mother, sister, and I attended Mass together on Easter morning. What a surprise I had when it was time to receive Communion. My parents stood and walked up the aisle with the rest of us! It was the first time I saw them receive Communion in all of my then-twenty-four years of life. My prayers had been answered! What a joy!

A month later my father died of a heart attack. But Jesus had answered my prayers. I saw my parents receive the Eucharist. I had prayed for that to happen all my life!

How had my parents been able to return to Jesus in the Eucharist? It was through the kind efforts of a friend of my brothers'. Two of my brothers had entered the seminary after eighth grade. Although neither of them ultimately decided to become priests, they made many friends while they were in the seminary. These seminarians would often come by our home and visit my parents when they were in Cumberland. It was on one of these home visits that one of my brothers' friends, who went on to be ordained, helped my parents through the process of returning to the sacraments.

I had never told anyone about the prayer I offered every day for my parents at the consecration of the sacred host. It was amazing that my father called and asked me to come home that Easter. He didn't know that I had been praying that he could return to the sacraments before he died. And neither of us knew that he only had one month left to live.

It was awesome to see how God answers our prayers with "yes," "no," or "in a little while"! God's time is not our time! In this case, "in a little while" was nearly a quarter of a century. But I kept on praying, and eventually I received my answer. I know that Jesus is present in the Eucharist and does hear and answer our prayers.

A Miracle in My Soul

by Maureen Sullivan

Like many other Catholics, I have been blessed with occasions of intimate communion with my Lord and Savior after receiving his precious body and blood during the holy sacrifice of the Mass. These moments are so special that I hold them quietly in my heart, knowing that I have done nothing to deserve this privilege.

Looking back, I treasure the poignant memory of my first Communion, which took place on a beautiful day in May. In the small group photo of six girls and four boys, I held my new white prayer book high for everyone to see. It mattered little that my two older sisters had worn the same dress and veil for their Communion days or that the dress would be passed on again to my younger sisters. All that mattered was what our class had been taught—namely, that on this special day a miracle was going to take place in our souls.

Sister had prepared us carefully and lovingly for this special event. First she explained that we needed to prepare our hearts to receive Jesus through the Sacrament of Reconciliation. Then she helped us to understand the great mystery of transubstantiation in very simple terms—that we were going to receive the actual body of Jesus on this joyous occasion.

Words could never describe the joy I felt that wonderful day, when I first received Jesus into my body. Sister was right—a miracle had indeed taken place in my soul. Over the years, although I admit I have questioned other aspects of my faith, I have never doubted the real presence of Jesus in the Eucharist.

Now in the twilight of my life, I feel blessed that the priests and deacons at my parish continue to celebrate Mass every day and offer Eucharistic adoration and benediction every week. The seeds of faith in the Eucharist that were planted when I was a young girl have grown into a conviction that I treasure and hold dear to my heart. That conviction is a true gift from God that no one can ever take from me.

Feeling Jesus Inside Me

by Dana Barber

As I continue to grow on my spiritual journey, the Year of the Eucharist has added new meaning to my life as a Catholic.

I will be forever grateful to the person who so persistently invited me to serve as an extraordinary minister of Holy Communion. My decision to become a part of this ministry took many months of thoughtful prayer. Although I eventually thought that I was ready to serve, nothing could have prepared me for the feelings I would experience. The first time I served, I felt as if I had been embraced by the Holy Spirit and shared a complete oneness with God. Every time I serve, this feeling is just as beautiful. And through this extraordinary ministry I am blessed to be able to share God's love with my family of faith.

Recently I was talking with a Christian friend about why Catholics believe that the Eucharist is truly the body and blood of Christ, and not simply a symbol. When I thought about the nature of my belief, what struck me is how differently I feel after receiving the Eucharist. The Eucharist provides nourishment that satisfies a hunger in my soul in a completely different way than ordinary food satisfies the hunger in my body. My heart also feels enlightened, as each reception of the Eucharist reveals a little more of the mystery of God's love. How fortunate we are as Catholics to be able to experience this wonderful gift.

And yet it was my nine-year-old son who summed it up best, without hesitation, and with the simplicity unique to a child. As

I was reflecting on what the Eucharist means to me, he turned to me said, "When I receive the body and blood of Christ I feel Jesus inside of me, and each time I feel more of his love growing in my heart!" At that moment I could just see the smile on Jesus' face. "I thank thee, Father, Lord of heaven and earth, that thou hast hidden these things from the wise and understanding and revealed them to babes" (Matthew 11:25).

Devotion to the Eucharist Is a Gift

by Chris Phillips

After engaging in Eucharistic adoration for nearly five years, I had no doubt that the Eucharist was central to my life. Reflecting on that fact should be a simple assignment, I thought—after all, I teach religious studies to high-school students! But when I began to ponder and pray about the reasons why the Eucharist means so much to me, the words did not come easily.

I considered perhaps sharing stories about the Lord's immediate answers to the prayers I have brought before him. Yet when I thought about his responses, I realized that they usually weren't that instantaneous. Many, in fact, were contrary to what I would have hoped for. And several may always be unclear to me. The Lord works in his own way and at his own time, and his agenda is not necessarily the same as our own. No, there weren't any fascinating stories here.

But the more I thought about it, the more I realized that my devotion to the Eucharist is as much a gift as the Eucharist itself—and one that I have taken for granted.

Why am I so devoted to the Eucharist? I intensely desire to be in love with God, and yet the fear of saying yes and committing myself to this relationship has always scared me. I have always been one to enter into prayer with all my petitions and, of course, to profess my love for God. But I am always tempted to put other people and concerns before him. My devotion to the Eucharist has helped me put things in perspective and see where God belongs in the order of my life.

I expected life to be rosy, but as we all eventually learn, it is often anything but. My devotion to the Eucharist is about life—which means that it is about love, forgiveness, understanding, and compassion. It is about becoming all of those things and incorporating them into my daily life. I know that there are limits to what I can do. I cannot change people or situations; I cannot make people more loving and prayerful. But through devotion to the Eucharist I can become Eucharist to those around me and have a transforming effect on others. I cannot make the world perfect. But through devotion to the Eucharist I can continue to realize what an incredible gift I have been given and how I am called to share it with others.

I know that I don't have all the answers. But I do know that through the Eucharist, God has given us an incredible gift. Through the presence of his Son, he calls all of us into a loving, committed relationship with him. God is always reaching out to us. And all we have to do is say yes.

Questions for Reflection

1. In what ways is the Eucharist a mystery? Have you ever found it a struggle to accept a mystery—something you couldn't explain in a scientific or rational way? How did you resolve your struggle?

2. Why do you think our heavenly Father desired to give us Jesus in the Eucharist? What does this gift say about God's nature? About God's love for us?

3. What practical steps could you or your family take to cultivate a deeper sense of gratitude for the Eucharist? In what ways could you express your gratitude to God?

CHAPTER 2
Transformation

The man who receives Holy
Communion loses himself in God
like a drop of water in the ocean: It's
impossible to separate them anymore.
. . . In these vast depths of love,
there's enough to lose yourself for
eternity.

—St. John Vianney

Finding My Center

by Marianne M. Faulstich

My husband of thirty-one years had a massive heart attack in September 2003. During the month he hovered between heaven and earth, I found myself crawling to Mass whenever it "fit in," as I juggled work and spending time with him in the ICU. Although I had been raised as a Catholic and attended Catholic schools, I had somehow missed the most important dimension of my faith. I followed my religious checklist well enough, but any spirituality I had was only about half an inch deep. My feeling was that God had more important things to do than get involved with my ordinary life, and that as long as I didn't screw up too badly, I was doing okay. Now my little world was crashing around me, and there was nothing I could do to stop it. So there I was, in the back of the church, quietly sobbing. But from somewhere deep within, I sensed a great hug of love, compassion, joy, peace, and calm. I had always believed that God loves us—humankind—in a nice, abstract sort of way. But for the first time in my life, I realized that God loves *me* and is with me "always" in "all ways." And I knew that everything would be okay. The feeling took my breath away.

After spending a month in the ICU, mostly unconscious, my husband died.

Slowly, I began to comprehend the meaning of the "communion of saints"—words I had mouthed since childhood, but had never really understood. God's presence (and my husband's), was most real for me when we gathered at the altar, so I tried to fit Mass into my life more often. My schedule left every other Friday free, so I started going to Mass on those days as well as on Saturdays. Lent came along, and I figured there was no harm in adding the other Friday. Then Holy Week, and I thought—Monday, Tuesday, and Wednesday before the Triduum—I could do that; I'd just adjust my schedule to a later shift for a while.

Our pastor suggested that since Easter lasts eight days, we might consider coming to Mass during the octave. After a few days, I told him that I would not be making a habit of daily Mass past Easter, because I did not want it to become routine. Things that become routine get taken for granted and fall into the humdrum of everyday life. I was learning to love the Mass and didn't want it to become one more item on a to-do list.

When I pondered this exchange later, I realized that Mass is not about me but about worship, and that it could only become routine if I let it. Maybe I should let God decide when he gets tired of seeing me, rather than the self-centered concern that I might get tired of Mass, or take it for granted, or not get a charge out of it. It's not about me . . . not about me . . . not about me. Some things were becoming clear: my life was being transformed in ways I had never dreamed possible. Nothing was the same anymore. I had a long way to go on this faith journey, and I was doing too much thinking. Or, perhaps, not enough?

A turning point came through a gospel I heard at Mass a couple of weeks after Easter. It takes place after the resurrection when the apostles, for lack of anything better to do, have gone back to fishing. They see Jesus on the shore cooking fish over a fire. I could almost smell it. He calls them to "come have breakfast." That line grabbed my heart like nothing I had experienced before. Breakfast—such a loving invitation. To make breakfast for someone usually means that you have to get up before they do, think about what they would like, and have it ready for them. You give up sleep and comfort and sometimes end a dream in order to provide nourishment for someone else. So what did this mean for me? I thought about how wonderful Jesus' invitation was. As far as I could remember, no man (including my husband!) had ever made me breakfast. Then I thought, "Wow, is Jesus talking to *me*? Is Jesus inviting *me* to come have breakfast with him every morning?"

I have been at Mass pretty much every day since then. Instead of fitting Mass into my life, I now fit my life around Mass. Is it routine? Yes and no. It is what I am; it is a habitual part of me and of my morning prayer. Is it boring, dry, ho-hum? No. Oh, God, no!

My heart has finally taken in what had previously only been in my head: That each Mass is the timeless sacrifice of the church that joins us to the perfect sacrifice of Jesus and allows us to share in the gift of his body and blood. That Mass is the one particular time and place where heaven touches earth. That Jesus is really and truly present, and that he loves me—personally. That he speaks to me and to my brothers and sisters through his word, feeds us with the Eucharist, and then sends us out to spread this good news to the world.

I have finally found what had been missing in my life. Each morning, Jesus, Lord of heaven and earth, becomes my breakfast, my nourishment, my spiritual food. He is the center of my life.

A Convert's Journey

by Norman Downs

I wasn't always a Catholic. In fact, it took a long journey to get where I am today. But I can assure you that it was well worth the trip.

I was baptized as an infant and grew up in a Protestant household. I knew the Apostles' Creed and the Lord's Prayer by heart, and for my confirmation I memorized the 23rd and 100th psalms.

Like many of my generation, as a young adult I gradually drifted away from my faith. For many years I did "my own thing" under the "spiritual" guidance of the Beatles, Jimi Hendrix, and the Rolling Stones. It was fun at first, but eventually my daily life became dreary and predictable. I had become spiritually bankrupt.

Then, sixteen years ago, I made a decision to change my life. As a direct result of a spiritual self-help group, I experienced a Christian conversion in an evangelical church. I have never been the same since. The evangelical conversion gave me a profound love for Jesus and the Scriptures. I desired to live my life to please and to serve God. But still I longed for more. I told my pastor that I wanted to know more about my Christian faith, and he suggested that I take evening classes at

St. Mary's Catholic Seminary, here in Baltimore.

About the same time that I was admitted to the Ecumenical Institute at St. Mary's, I was also seeking some quiet time away from the world. A friend who is a Presbyterian minister suggested I make a retreat at an Anglican convent and retreat center near Baltimore. The experience of the convent was beautiful and holy. I became acquainted with Catholic spirituality there and at St. Mary's. As a Protestant I had always understood a personal, immanent Jesus. But now I also came to know a transcendent and majestic Jesus. I became fascinated with symbol, liturgy, and last but not least, the Eucharist.

I sensed that our Lord was calling me to change. I wasn't ready yet to become Catholic, so I chose a Protestant denomination similar to Catholicism and similar to the one I grew up in. There I learned more about the Christian liturgical year, the symbols of the faith, and the Eucharist.

A local church offered Communion every day, and I went with great enthusiasm. I didn't know what was happening as I found myself drawn to the Lord's Supper. A friend even asked me what I was doing differently that made me seem more grounded and stable. The only answer I could come up with was frequent reception of Communion, a practice embraced by many of the saints of the Catholic Church. As I studied the Bible I learned that the Eucharist, and not only the preached word of God, was the center of Catholic worship. Scripture verses such as, "I am the bread of life; he who comes to me shall not hunger, and he who believes in me shall never thirst" (John 6:35), really spoke to me. Other verses convinced me of the prominence of the Eucharist. The Acts of the Apostles says that those who were baptized "devoted themselves to the apostles' teaching and fellowship, to the breaking of bread and the prayers" (Acts 2:42). St. Paul says,

> For I received from the Lord what I also delivered to you, that the Lord Jesus on the night when he was betrayed took bread, and when he had given thanks, he broke it, and said, "This is my body which is for you. Do this in remembrance of me." In the same way also the cup, after supper, saying, "This cup is the new covenant in my blood. Do this, as often as you drink it, in remembrance of me." For as often as you eat this bread and drink the cup, you proclaim the Lord's death until he comes. (1 Corinthians 11:23-26)

The statement "for I received from the Lord what I also delivered to you" is only used one other time by St. Paul in the New Testament. Later in First Corinthians he explains that what he has handed on "as of first importance" is "that Christ died for our sins, . . . that he was buried, [and] that he was raised on the third day" (15:3-4). It seems pretty clear to me that the Eucharist is essential for Christian life and salvation.

It was only a matter of time before I thirsted to become a Catholic. I wanted to stay in the comfort of my Protestant tradition, with its elegant and beautiful liturgies and music. But Jesus always calls us higher. As I explored Catholic Masses, benediction services, and perpetual adoration, the pull on me became even stronger. I became fully convinced of the truth of

Catholic teachings. The Eucharist is not merely symbolic, but is Jesus' gift to us of his very flesh. I wanted to receive Jesus in the Eucharist, but I respected the rules for receiving Communion in Catholic churches.

Finally I took RCIA classes, and on April 19, 2003, I was confirmed, received my first Communion, and was welcomed into the church. The conversion was life changing. I was at last able to receive the actual body and blood of Christ in the Eucharist and feel the love and joy of Jesus Christ as a part of the church he founded. The Eucharist is vital and central to my faith. It is my spiritual nourishment.

I am excited and at times apprehensive about what the future will hold. Our Lord continues to call us to work in his vineyard, and I don't know where he will lead me next. But I do know I cannot live without the Eucharist as I "grow in the grace and knowledge of our Lord and Savior Jesus Christ" (2 Peter 3:18).

Return from Hopelessness

by Carmen M. Arroyo

Life is full of surprises. Although I had been blessed with a loving Christian family, a good education, and a prestigious job, about three years ago I developed a chronic disease that changed my life forever. In my hopelessness, I decided to make a more serious commitment to my Catholic faith. Previously I had gone to Mass only on Sundays, but I started to attend

Mass and receive the Eucharist every day. Going to Mass every day really transformed me. I had been a very demanding and arrogant person, but I realized that our Lord was making me more compassionate and humble.

I now realize that there are three things we must do in life, which I call the "three L's." We must

Love—Love God and one another as our Lord Jesus told us;

Laugh—Even if we are sad, we should rejoice in our Lord Jesus; and

Listen—We must listen to the Holy Spirit and to others.

The way our Lord has transformed me is a miracle of love—the miracle of the Eucharist. Thank you, God.

A Child Shall Lead

by Barbara Coakley

In the late 1960s, I taught sixth grade at Most Holy Rosary School in Syracuse, New York. Every Tuesday afternoon we had early dismissal so that the Catholic children attending nearby public schools could come to us for their religious instruction. At the request of our director of religious education, I was to prepare a class of about fifty second-graders to receive their first Holy Communion, so every Tuesday afternoon the large desks in my classroom were occupied by small seven-year-olds.

Two special memories remain in my mind and heart from that challenging yet awesome experience. One is the time I stood before the class, attempting to explain the presence of Jesus in the Eucharist. Making a circle with my right thumb and index finger, I proclaimed, "I know it's hard for you to believe this, but the small host that looks and tastes like bread is really the body and blood of Christ." From the mouth of one of the little guys came the words, "I don't think it's hard to believe; I believe it!" The rest of the class smiled in agreement. My faith was renewed by a little child.

The second memory comes from that same class on the day of their first Communion, the first Saturday in May. Even though we had started instruction in September, with so many students in the class I was lucky if I knew all of their names by May, let alone their readiness to receive our blessed Lord. Whether they were ready or not, their special day arrived. It was with a mother's pride that I watched them walk reverently to the Communion rail. (In those days a railing separated the priest from the communicants, so the children knelt side by side with their hands folded, waiting anxiously to partake of the Holy Eucharist.) My pride soon vanished when I saw my star pupil, Tina, begin to cry and cover her sweet face with her hands. I immediately directed this prayer to our heavenly Father: "Lord, she was the best kid in the class. Why is this happening? Please let her stop crying and receive your divine Son!" Since Tina continued to cry, I thought that God wasn't listening, and my faith was definitely faltering. Tina kept her face covered until her mother came up and took her back to her seat to comfort her.

After Mass, while our celebrant was outside getting his picture taken with the numerous communicants, Tina's mother approached me. She said that Tina was nervous in front of everyone, and she wondered if Father would come back into the church, to give herself *and* Tina Holy Communion. She felt that Tina might be more willing to receive Communion if she did, too. Knowing our priest, I assured her that he would gladly respond to her request. Then she humbly added, "Would you ask him if he would hear *my* confession first? I haven't received Communion for several years." It was then I knew that God's plan was not for Tina to receive him that day but to prepare the way for her mother to return to him. It wasn't until the following Sunday that I witnessed Tina's first Communion, as she led her mother back to the altar with her.

Forty years have passed since those children strengthened my faith and brought me to a deeper union with Christ. May God's children continue to lead others back to him, and may each Communion bring us closer to an eternal union with him.

The Light of Christ

by Veronica Zipp

To say that the Eucharist has transformed my life would be an understatement. But the faith in Christ's presence that burns brightly in me now started out as a mere flicker. Even after twelve years of Catholic education, I don't think I truly believed that Jesus was present in the Eucharist. In fact, it wasn't until my mid-thirties that I began to have a real change of mind and heart.

I am grateful for all the wonderful mentors the Holy Spirit has provided over the years to help fan the flames of my faith. Through their actions as well as their words, these people have truly been "Eucharist" to me by revealing the real presence of Christ.

One of those friends once told me that his love for Jesus in the Eucharist is the reason he goes to Mass every day. "After all," he asked, "doesn't everyone want to be with the one they love?"

That question got me thinking, and I started going to daily Mass whenever I wasn't at work. As a result, the Mass became the focal point of my life. I wonder now how I could possibly function as a Catholic—evangelizing and ministering to others—if Jesus was not within me spiritually and physically.

Jesus loves us and longs to be with us, too. And we are free to reject his love. "How would your spouse and children feel," another friend asked, "if you didn't spend time with them?"

Perhaps you have experienced the pain of not being loved, yourself. But have you ever experienced the grief of loving someone and having your love rejected? Jesus loves us so intensely that he gave his life for us on the cross so that we would turn away from sin and be with him forever. We didn't do anything to deserve his love; he gives it to us freely. But just imagine how Jesus feels when we don't accept his love.

To show Jesus how grateful I am for his love, I began to spend time in Eucharistic adoration, pouring out my heart to him. I can't tell you how much healing I have experienced just by sitting in Jesus' presence. I truly believe that if the person with the hardest heart would go faithfully before Jesus in the

Eucharist, that person's heart would be changed. It would be impossible for it to remain hardened!

Jesus' presence in the Eucharist is a healing presence, too. Through the Eucharist, we touch the hem of the garment. A priest once suggested that when people come to receive Communion, they should bring to Jesus anything that is in need of healing. At one point in my life, I was overcome by an overwhelming sense of fear and worry to the point that it was consuming me. I asked Jesus in the Eucharist, "If it be your will, please take this from me; but if it is not, please let me know that my suffering is not useless." Jesus healed me and removed my anxiety. I hadn't done anything to make it go away; the situation that I thought had caused it was still there. But the fear and worry I had experienced were gone!

I am now a Eucharistic minister. What an incredible privilege and honor it is for me to be able to bring the presence of Christ to others!

I found out that faith is not about how smart you are, or what degrees you have, because I have none of that! But it is about an open heart, and everyone is capable of giving their heart to God. It's about using what God gave you and not looking to the right or left, but keeping your eyes fixed on him.

I am grateful for God's mercies in my life. I am grateful to the Holy Spirit for leading me closer to Jesus and to a deeper awareness and understanding of my Catholic faith.

It is still unfathomable to me how humble our God is that he would come to us in such an intimate way. What would life be like if every Catholic lived the Eucharist? We would truly be "the light of the world . . . a city set on a hill"

(Matthew 5:14). Then we would see a change in our families and in the world.

The Eucharist is power! It's our food to sustain us in this life and our food to lead us into the next life. In Jesus we can do all things. May God place a spark in our hearts, and may the Holy Spirit fan the flame until we all burn brightly as one!

My Prayer

by Sherry Rhodes

As I briefly held you in my hands this morning, I felt the wonder of the moment. My God and Savior, soon to be in my heart, momentarily resting in my hand, coming to dwell in my unworthy abode.

I wanted to understand and marvel at the magnificence of this moment, to have time to know, as some of the saints have known, the true enormity of this event: God opening himself up to me, waiting for me to invite him into my body and soul. It is a mystery too vast for my tiny mind to comprehend, so I go to the Eucharist unprepared for the magnitude of the experience that awaits me.

Jesus, you become one with me. You come into this creature, this unformed being. You, the King, take up residence in the humblest cottage of my heart. How unfit for a king is this vessel, let alone for my God. You wait for me to come and take you away to my heart—you actually wait for this event. You desire to come to this most unworthy servant.

My wish has always been that I could come to you. In you I could hide, safe from all of my weaknesses. I could retreat from all temptations and rest peacefully in the strength of my God. You wouldn't even have to acknowledge my presence. I could stay in some little corner of your being and find comfort in the complete joy of knowing that I am with you each moment.

But I *am* with you each moment, because you have chosen to come and dwell in me. So, dear Jesus, I will run with joy to receive you each day. And I will pray that as you come into me you will change me, so that some day I might have your heart in me.

Questions for Reflection

1. Why should we have expectant faith that through our reception of the Eucharist, Jesus will transform us? What, if any, obstacles prevent you from fully believing in the transforming power of the Eucharist?

2. Look back over your life and reflect on the ways that the Lord has transformed you. In what ways is your heart more like that of Jesus than it was several years ago? In what areas of your life do you still see the need for transformation?

3. Do you ever fear the possible changes in your life that might occur if you allowed Jesus to transform you? Why or why not?

CHAPTER 3

Presence

Every day he humbles himself just as he did when he came from his heavenly throne into the Virgin's womb; every day he comes to us and lets us see him in lowliness, when he descends from the bosom of the Father into the hands of the priest at the altar.

—St. Francis of Assisi

Kevin and His Best Friend

by Rebecca Drinks

Oh, no! The "cry rooms" at St. Joseph Church in Fullerton, Maryland, were filled to capacity! Now the only option was the balcony, where my son Kevin's exclamations were sure to echo throughout the church. I resolved to leave and attend a separate Mass if Kevin became too disruptive, but in the meantime, with the help of my husband Paul and our son Eric, I ushered Kevin up the steps.

Kevin, who was nine at the time, is autistic. Because of this neurological disorder, he is in constant motion, often uttering cries of excitement or irritation. Throughout the Mass, we continually asked Kevin to sit down and be quiet and tried to get him to focus a few seconds on the hymnal or missal. Little did we suspect that an unforgettable moment was approaching.

Kevin had received his first Communion a few years earlier, thanks to the loving instruction of Miss Joanne and Miss Brenda, special educators at St. Stephen's Church. In spite of the fact that Kevin's vocabulary consisted of approximately twenty short phrases dealing mainly with food items, he had learned from Miss Joanne to respond, "Amen," when given the body of Christ; and whenever he heard the word "Jesus," he immediately replied, "is my best friend."

As usual, when the time arrived for the priest to elevate the host during the consecration, I turned to Kevin to whisper, "Jesus." However, what I saw convinced me that no words were necessary. Kevin had ceased all squirming and vocalizations. As the host was raised, he immediately stood on the kneeler and gazed down at the altar. His eyes widened and darted back and forth from one side of the altar to the other. His face glowed with an expression of pure joy. His body remained motionless. Paul, Eric, and I looked at Kevin and then at each other. As we later learned, we all shared the same thought—that Kevin was seeing something sublimely beautiful and captivating that no one else could see. As his eyes darted back and forth, we imagined that he was seeing angels and the communion of saints gathered around the altar. As soon as the consecration ended, Kevin plopped down on the pew and resumed his normally active, autistic behavior.

We will always remember this rare glimpse of a beautiful, innocent soul enthralled with a heavenly vision of the Eucharist at consecration—the body, blood, soul, and divinity of Kevin's "best friend."

In the Company of Angels

by Sandy Korzick

In 1985, at the request of Fr. Jim Barker, I became an extraordinary minister of Holy Communion at St. Joseph Church in Cockeysville, Maryland. Several years later, as a Lenten goal, I decided to attend the 7:00 a.m. Mass each day. While I was going to Mass every day, I became aware of positive changes in myself. Even others noticed that my outlook had improved. When Lent was over, I stopped going to daily

Mass, but I quickly realized how much I missed starting my day with Mass and how wonderful I felt when I received the Blessed Sacrament. So I went back to daily Mass and signed up to serve as a Eucharistic minister on specific weekdays.

Over the next ten years, the Lord blessed my life in many ways, and I was privileged to witness several extraordinary events that I knew only God could bring about. Over the years, as my prayer life also grew, one of my prayer requests had become a desire to know that Jesus is truly present in the Blessed Sacrament. I know that the apostle Thomas and I have much in common, and I'm sure St. Thomas must have enjoyed seeing what our Lord had in store for me on the first Tuesday in August 1995.

Ready to assume my role as the minister of the cup at Mass, I positioned myself behind and to the left of our celebrant, Fr. Bernard Bak, at the breaking of the bread. Fr. Bak turned to me, and I received the sacred host into my extended hands. After seeing that Fr. Bak had consumed our Lord's body, I started to raise the Blessed Sacrament toward my mouth.

What happened next was nothing short of astounding. Before the sacred host had reached my lips, a flash suddenly went off before my eyes, like the flash from a camera. Within that momentary flash I saw the visible faces and upper bodies of two angels that were bending with prayerful hands raised in complete adoration to what I was bringing to my mouth. Behind them were countless more angels, less visible, but also in a posture of profound adoration. In as brief an instant the vision was gone, and I was left trembling all over and fighting back the tears that now flooded my eyes.

The minutes that followed are like a blur. I thought for sure that Fr. Bak must have noticed my trembling and look of astonishment when he presented the chalice to me. I've often wondered if my astonished look, tearing eyes, and shaking hands were apparent to other communicants as I completed my special role that morning. I returned to my seat to offer the most profound thanksgiving I believe I have ever given in my life.

After Mass I quickly found Fr. Bak in the sacristy and collapsed in a tearful heap as I began to tell him what had just happened at the altar. Fr. Bak had no problem believing that my experience was real and told me that God had heard my prayers and given me a sign. Just as St. Thomas did, I can now without any doubt fervently proclaim, "My Lord and my God!" and receive with awesome *joy* what the adoring angels long to receive but cannot. Oh, what a gift we receive, but how often we fail to recognize or truly appreciate how truly *wonderful* it is.

My Traveling Companion

by Mary C. Kerr Orndorff

I had always wanted to travel to Europe, and so I decided to go on a three-country European tour recently, even though I wouldn't know anyone in the group. I met several delightful people on the trip, of course, and had a wonderful time. And to my delight, I also discovered that I had a traveling companion all along that I both knew and loved—our Lord Jesus, present in the Eucharist.

France was the first country on the tour, and our first stop was Notre Dame Cathedral in Paris. Inside, the wide side aisles accommodated several tour groups. We were quietly making the rounds admiring the stained-glass windows and stunning architecture, when suddenly I heard the tinkle of a bell at the front of the cathedral and realized that Mass was being celebrated. I hurried to the spot in the sanctuary where Communion was being distributed, but the guard wouldn't let me through. She tried to tell me in French that Mass was going on, and I tried to explain with halting French and hand gestures that I wanted to attend the Mass. She soon understood and unlatched the heavy red-velvet cord, allowing me to enter. Was I ever happy! My first stop in a foreign country—how could I be so lucky! Now I had Jesus as my companion.

In Spain we had an opportunity to do some exploring on our own. As I browsed the side streets in Madrid one morning, I happened upon a small church. Because of the hot day the door was open, and I saw that Mass was starting. So once again I had the privilege of receiving the Eucharist.

On the visit to Ireland, while I was waiting in line to kiss the Blarney Stone, I heard the sound of church bells. I thought that they might have been playing the Angelus, so I went closer to find out. I crossed the little rural road and made my way up the hill to the church. Sure enough, a Mass was underway. It seemed that Jesus in the Blessed Sacrament was always inviting me to come to him.

What a wonderful trip! Talk about the luck of the Irish—I didn't even miss daily Mass. (You might be interested to know that I did get to kiss the Blarney Stone.) I will always remember the experience of visiting those beautiful places. But the trip just wouldn't have been the same without my beloved "traveling companion."

"In Your Presence, Lord"

by Pauline Tebo, SFO

As I sat before the Blessed Sacrament at St. Margaret Chapel in Bel Air, I found myself slipping into a deep meditation. I remained in that state for what seemed to be hours. It wasn't the first time that I found myself in a meditative state at the exposition of the Blessed Sacrament.

I'm a poet and song lyricist. Words often pop into my head at unusual times. I usually have a notepad with me to write the snippets down so I won't forget them. But on this particular day, it was different. I heard an internal voice telling me to write down the words. At first, I ignored the voice, but its gentle persistence led me to believe that it was the Holy Spirit speaking to me.

Wouldn't you know I had no notepad, no paper of any kind on which to jot down the message. I frantically looked around the pew for something to write on. Then, tucked inside a nearby hymnal, I noticed a weekly bulletin that had been left behind. I began to write down every word I was hearing. In a few moments the voice ceased, and an overwhelming feeling of peace came over me.

I read over the lyrics that had just been given to me and realized that they were even metered properly. I have no technical musical training, so I contacted someone I knew who might be able to help me put music to the words. Doug Kingsley from St. Ursula's Parish studied the lyrics and prayed for several months before committing any notes to paper, but the result was one of inspiration. "In Your Presence, Lord" was born.

There is something special about this particular song for me. I'd never written lyrics before that required no changes or adjustments in either tempo or thought.

Of course, I hope that someday this piece will be published. But so far, no interest has been forthcoming from any music publisher. I would also love to hear it sung by a grand choir, but even if that never happens, I know for once that I was obedient to God and wrote the words exactly as he gave them to me.

I was merely a tool and can take no credit for the content of this song, but it gives me great joy to look at the words and know that the message is from God.

In Your Presence, Lord

In Your presence, Lord, I ask for forgiveness.
In Your presence, Lord, I offer you my prayer,
    that You send Your Spirit to one who is not worthy
    to be . . . in Your presence.
In Your presence, Lord, my eyes gaze upon you.

In Your presence, Lord, my heart fills with joy,
>that You chose to love me knowing I'm not worthy
>to be . . . in Your presence.
As I kneel before you deep in adoration,
I feel your love reach out . . . touching me,
>filling me with strength.
In Your presence, Lord, Your peace lives within me.
In Your presence, Lord, I'm humbled once again.
If I live within You then, now and forever
>I'll be . . . in Your presence.

(© Pauline Tebo—Lyrics 1998; © Doug J. Kingsley—Music 2000)

The Eyes to See Jesus

by Kathy Haynes

How often we are present at the celebration of the Eucharist, yet how seldom we are fully aware of the great mystery taking place right before our eyes!

I was meditating before the start of Mass one day on how lucky the apostles were to have shared the Last Supper with Jesus. What a great privilege to have received the bread and wine from his own hands and to have known him, to have been able to reach out and touch him, to converse with him and actually hear his responses. How fortunate they were to be that close to the Son of God! How I longed for the certainty that came from seeing him, hearing him, touching him in the flesh. How truly he was Emmanuel—"God with us"—during his earthly life. But how distant he can seem now, after the intervening two thousand years.

Such was the direction my meditation was taking—what I termed "apostle envy." Then, under the guidance of the Holy Spirit, my meditation took a different turn. At the Last Supper the apostles still didn't really understand who Jesus was or the nature of the gift he was about to give them. In fact, they may have had less of an idea than I do, despite their having seen, heard, and walked with him. The suffering Messiah was not what they were expecting; they were expecting an earthly king. They were not expecting a servant; they were expecting a leader. Was he divine? Was he human? These were issues the early Christian church wrestled with in the first centuries after the incarnation.

During the consecration I was suddenly transported outside of time to view the past two thousand years, and I experienced how I was connected through history not only to the original Last Supper but to all Christians in all generations who had faithfully celebrated that event. I experienced the union that awaits all of us in the communion of saints. For a brief moment I was celebrating the Eucharist with St. Francis of Assisi, St. John Bosco, and with devout Christians from all over the world throughout history, experiencing the myriad local adaptations to the one unchanging mystery. Then just as suddenly I was back in my own church, surrounded by my friends and neighbors, back in the twenty-first century.

God's revelation was completed in Jesus. However, our understanding of that revelation is still unfolding under the guidance of the Holy Spirit. The same Spirit that came to

Jesus' followers at Pentecost still comes to his followers today. I realize now that the apostles, the early Christians, and Christians right up to the present day still wrestle with who Jesus is. Only now I am thankful to have the two-thousand-year Catholic tradition to help me interpret who Jesus is. Jesus still comes to us in the bread and wine. He is no more hidden and no more obvious in the bread and wine than he was in the flesh. He still comes to those who have eyes to see.

In His Presence Always

by Charlotte A. Taylor

Have you ever felt uplifted after just being in the same room with a person? It doesn't have to be someone you know—maybe a person you have just met—and there doesn't need to be much conversation. Somehow, the presence of that woman or man gives you a psychological or spiritual lift—a "high," so to speak. It is always a wonderful feeling, and I assume it has something to do with the presence of God in that person.

For many years, whenever I've driven past a Catholic church or a Blessed Sacrament chapel, I've mentally sent a brief greeting to our Lord in the tabernacle. One day, when I was in a fast-food restaurant with my good friend and our active children, who were in our booth climbing all over us, I remembered that the Cathedral of St. Thomas More in Arlington, Virginia, was only a block away. So despite the distractions of the kids, I mentally sent my usual greeting to our Lord.

The following week my husband and I were driving past the same fast-food eatery. Since we were so close to the cathedral, I again sent our Savior a greeting. Then I had a thought that must have come from the Holy Spirit: When we drive by the home of a friend without stopping, he or she probably doesn't even realize it, but when we drive past our Lord's residence (and he has many) and acknowledge his presence, he always knows. At that point I experienced the greatest sense of Jesus' presence I had ever felt. It seemed that he was sitting in the front seat of the car between my husband and me. Talk about a high—this one lasted for five days!

Years later I mentioned my experience to my dear friend Myra, a contemplative nun. She asked if I realized how much our Lord appreciates being remembered in this way. I had never thought of that before. In the Blessed Sacrament, Jesus gives us the gift of his very self and shows us his desire to be with us always. To greet our Lord at his "home" in the tabernacle—or even when we're just driving by—is to experience his presence with us.

Questions for Reflection

1. Surveys have shown that some Catholics find it difficult to believe in the real presence of Christ in the Eucharist. How would you advise someone who is finding this belief a stumbling block?

2. How often do you find yourself desiring to praise God during Mass? Why would praise be a fitting response to the reality of Christ's presence in the Eucharist? How would the image of angels gathered around the altar help you?

3. Christ's presence is "hidden" under the species of bread and wine. How does recognition of Jesus in the Eucharist help us to see Christ in our loved ones? In the poor, the sick, and the imprisoned? In prayer and Scripture? How can the Eucharist help us to deepen our appreciation of Jesus' presence as we go about our day?

CHAPTER 4

Adoration

Do you realize that Jesus is there in the tabernacle expressly for you, for you *alone*? He burns with the desire to come into your heart.

—St. Thérèse of Lisieux

Discovering the Real Event

by Karen Wingard

When Pope John Paul II came to Baltimore in October 1995, our whole family was able to go to see him. Even with the distractions of the crowd, when the pope entered the stadium at Camden Yards, there was a tangible sense of God's presence that seemed to emanate from him. It created a longing in me; I didn't want him to leave.

So when I learned that the pope was coming to Toronto for World Youth Day in 2002, I made plans to attend. I looked forward to that same experience of God's presence again. I traveled to Canada that July with two of our daughters and joined the throngs of young people from around the world. The Exhibition Place, which hosted the afternoon and evening events, is nearly a mile in length. Even so, the area was packed. We enjoyed walking its length, watching the various youth groups with their colorful banners coming and going.

Larger church groups stayed in church halls, but since we were a small group of three, we stayed at the home of a Toronto family. Our hostess fed us well and entertained us with stories. After long days attending World Youth Day activities, we returned in the evenings to watch news of the event on TV. We saw the pope's arrival, his greeting of a young girl, and his lunch with a group of people with disabilities. During the first couple of days, I felt that all of Toronto was seeing more of the pope on TV than we did at World Youth Day. Soon, however, we would have our chance, with the official welcome of the pope on Thursday, July 25.

Thursday came, and there was free time before the pope's arrival, so I decided that we should visit the famous CN Tower. Many others had the same idea; the line was long. We paid extra for special tickets that shortened the wait. The view from the top was wonderful. We could see the park and observed the crowd swelling below. Gradually, it dawned on me that it would take more time to descend the tower than I had allotted. When we hit the street, all the trolleys were full, so we joined others hurrying on foot to the park. We would get there in time for the motorcade, but too late to get a good spot on the pope's route. As we approached the park, we entered the screened-in overflow section, where confessions were being offered, and we heard the pope speaking. The procession had finished, and he was already partway through his greeting! We were missing the whole thing. What had happened? A fellow pilgrim explained that the pope had been so eager to meet us that he had arrived an hour early!

Pope John Paul finished his speech, and the motorcade exited at the far end of the park. I was crushed. All the planning, all the driving, the press of the crowds, the long commutes into town each day, the exhaustion—all for nothing! I had missed it. And it was my own fault! I struggled with extreme frustration. Perhaps I would be near him at the papal Mass Sunday morning. But still . . . !

The girls and I wandered aimlessly through the crowd. Eventually we came to the far end of the park, where the dancing had been earlier. Along the way, we stopped at several indoor events. As we approached the hall, I noticed a banner over the doors of another building. It announced, "Eucharistic Adoration." I hadn't noticed it there before.

The wide doorway was open. Inside I saw a cold, gray concrete floor covered with small pads for kneeling, a crowd of people, a group singing loudly, a table with candles, and a monstrance rising above the candles. As we entered this makeshift chapel, I was overcome with the same tangible presence of God that I had experienced years before at Camden Yards. But this time it was even stronger, warmer, more "real." Immersed in the presence of God, I knelt; nothing else mattered. I felt a strong reassurance: "I AM. I AM the One you seek. I AM the reality." The love of Jesus kept washing over me. I realized that it was Jesus, not the pope, that my heart really longed for, and Jesus was filling me with his love. I hadn't missed what I was looking for, after all. "In thy presence there is fulness of joy" (Psalm 16:11). I had never had anything so real; God had never been so present as at that moment.

In past years, I had been "born again"; I had been part of Bible studies, prayer groups, and the Charismatic Renewal; and I had attended conferences, retreats, and praise sessions. But never had I encountered my Lord so powerfully or so intimately as I did that afternoon in 2002. I loved Pope John Paul II; he was a holy person, and in his presence I sensed the presence of God. I didn't get to see the pope that day; I got something even better. Our Lord graciously revealed himself to me in the Eucharist. It was the most powerful experience of my life.

Falling Back to God

by Emily Yount, age 15

I have heard of people who have been touched by God during adoration of the Blessed Sacrament. I just didn't know that I would be one of them. It happened on my confirmation retreat this past January. I had been on other retreats before, but none of them had ever affected me like this one.

I had been really depressed before the confirmation retreat, because I have SAD (Seasonal Affective Disorder), which is always the worst in the wintertime. I felt really far from God. It was hard for me to even think that he was real. I knew I believed in something, but I just didn't know what it was.

When it was time for adoration of the Eucharist, I just sat there at first, watching everyone and listening to them cry. I was just thinking for a while, when I decided that I would touch the monstrance. When I did, it felt like God just went right through me. It was a little scary!

I went back to my spot and I prayed. I asked God questions about the past and wondered why he hadn't been there for me. That's how it felt to me, anyway. I started to think that questioning God about things and yelling at him inside my head wasn't a good idea. It seemed like it wasn't working, either. So, I decided that I would ask him to come back into my life and apologize to him for how I had been in the past. I kept repeating this prayer over and over, until I started to get weak and felt like I was going to fall. I tried to stay up. Finally I couldn't take it anymore, and I fell. Someone caught me, and others began to pray around me. It was a very moving experience.

Going into a peaceful state like that is the best thing that ever happened to me. After that day, I realized that there still is and always was a God, and that he will always be there for me no matter what I do. I like to think that my experience was a sign of my maturity, because even though I was practically Godless at the time, I still asked God to come back to me.

Perpetual Adoration, Perpetual Love

by Dana Hilmoe

It is difficult to put into words the incredible effect that my weekly trips to the adoration chapel have had on my life.

Shortly before the chapel opened, a priest came to Mass and explained that the Blessed Sacrament would be exposed in the chapel around the clock, seven days a week, all year long, and that parishioners would be asked to sign up for hourly adoration.

I was by myself at Mass on this particular Sunday, a very odd occurrence for a mother of four young children. The ushers distributed forms for us to fill out if we wanted to participate in adoration. I have to admit that I was hesitant to sign up. But when the usher looked at me to collect my paper, I felt moved by the Holy Spirit to write my name. I really had no understanding of what I was about to experience.

A couple of weeks went by, and I gave little thought to signing up for adoration until I received a phone call regarding my hour and day. Once I was on the phone with the hourly coordinator, I felt that it was impossible to refuse—which I interpreted as a clear sign that the Lord was drawing me to him. When I hung up the phone, I was hit with the realization that I had just committed myself to "perpetual adoration." "Perpetual"—meaning "forever."

When I arrived at the adoration chapel at my appointed time on that first Saturday almost six years ago, I was in awe of the Lord's presence before me. I began to speak to him, and he led me to a deeper, fuller understanding of my Catholic faith.

I have prayed for many things over the course of the last six years, and I feel that the Lord has been ever present to me. I prayed for my brother's return to the church, for his son's baptism, and for a closer bond among my brother and his wife and son, my parents, and my family. In time, all of these prayers were answered. Not only did my brother return to the church and baptize his son, but my formerly Jewish sister-in-law was moved to explore her husband's faith and eventually become a Catholic.

Also during the last six years, my father was diagnosed with stage-three lung cancer. Every Saturday I asked the Lord to heal him and to guide the physicians who cared for him. I prayed through the intercession of St. Peregrine that my father would be well again. Once again, the Lord answered my prayers. My father is now nearing three years in remission.

I know that not all of my prayers will be answered and that God has a particular plan for me and for my life. Each week I pray that I may find God in my life and that I may do his work as he leads me. I try to pray as Jesus did that his will, not mine, be done in my life. Wherever life takes me, I know that God will be leading me. The Holy Spirit draws me closer to him each week in the gift of the adoration chapel.

A Convert's Story

by Anne Merwin

As a child, I loved going to our Protestant church on Sundays. I loved hearing the beautiful prayers and hymns. While I was growing up, I visited many great English cathedrals with my family, and I remember being filled with wonder at the majesty of those structures. They always made me feel uplifted.

And yet, the historic tombs and floors of those great cathedrals were cold and a little too final. I knew that God was in the cathedrals and in my church, but I couldn't pinpoint where he was. Somehow God seemed more magnificent outdoors. I remember one especially powerful experience. Near the wild shores of Cape Cod, I looked up at the expansive sky and recognized there the mighty power of God. As my eyes traveled up to the sky, down to the blue ocean, across the fields, and all around me, I realized that God's greatness was endless. Nature was overwhelming me, and God was in all of it.

As a young adult, I felt a need for God to play a larger role in my life. I attended church services regularly, enrolled in Bible studies, went on retreats, participated in prayer meetings, and prayed on my own. But no matter what I did, I felt that I was forcing myself to stay in God's presence, as if my connection with him was all too fragile.

Then one day while praying in a church in Boston, I understood that God was indeed my Father. I realized then that no matter what happened, God would be with me and I could depend on him. This newfound relationship I felt with my heavenly Father helped me look at the Catholic Church with new eyes. Why did Catholics receive Communion at every Mass? Why wasn't once a month enough? I felt that I had to learn more about the Eucharist.

After much study and preparation, I converted to Roman Catholicism. However, I felt overwhelmed. The Catholic Church offered many devotions and prayers, and it was difficult to know where to start. At first I would kneel in empty churches in front of the Blessed Sacrament and pray. There was something comforting about being there, and I found it easier to pray in those surroundings. The Eucharist was more meaningful to me now, but still I felt that something was missing. It was as if I was floating offshore while God was on land. Some days I would make progress and get nearer to God, only to be washed backwards again by waves of anxiety or other obstacles to my faith.

Then shortly after I moved to Baltimore, God provided two opportunities for me to connect to him. The first was learning about the life of Elizabeth Ann Seton, the first U.S. native saint. I discovered that the Eucharist had helped to draw her to Catholicism. I was fascinated. The more I learned about Elizabeth Seton, the more I learned about my Catholic faith.

Her example helped to prepare me for the most moving

spiritual experience of my life—which was the second opportunity God gave me. It happened several years later, while I was attending Holy Thursday Mass at the Cathedral of Mary Our Queen in Baltimore. After Mass people started filing into the Blessed Sacrament chapel for veneration. I was reluctant to leave my seat right away, however, because the organ's lingering notes of "Stay with Me" were so beautiful. So I made my way slowly down the aisle to the chapel. Inside, people were already kneeling in hushed adoration. I looked at the altar, and suddenly something in my soul seemed to burst into flames. All I could think was, "Here is all beauty; nothing could be more perfect anywhere."

So this was the Eucharist. Finally, I understood.

For the past eight or so years, I have visited the Blessed Sacrament as if I was going home. There is always warmth, comfort, and peace in its presence. The consecration during Mass often helps to melt the hardening of my heart. The fire of the Holy Spirit is real. And God, who was always with me even when I didn't feel quite connected with him, has given me the presence of his Son in the Eucharist to forge the bond. In the presence of the Eucharist, there is pure hope, pure peace, and pure joy.

This past Holy Thursday, during Eucharistic adoration, I thought about the face of Jesus surrounded by the crown of thorns. The crown encircled his face so that I could clearly see every thorn. Then the thorns were transformed into the rays of the monstrance with the Eucharist as its center. To me, the thorns that mocked Jesus and made him suffer for my sake became rays of light and hope through his gift of the Eucharist. So my response to the Eucharist can only be gratitude. God has given me the most perfect gift of all, the gift of his Son, and the ability to fully understand that gift through the Eucharist.

To bring the peace that the Eucharist gives me to my daily life is my greatest challenge. The eyes of Jesus reflect my soul with all its shortcomings. But there is also acceptance, love, and hope in those eyes. Thus I can hope to finish my journey eventually, eternally with Christ. Until then, the Eucharist will help me when I stray off the path to my eternal home.

An Adoration Prayer

Merciful Lord, forgive me.
Gentle Lord, free and heal me.
All-knowing Lord, strengthen my soul.
Glorious Lord, nourish me.
Loving Lord, lift up my eyes and lead me.
Heavenly Father, you are my hope and my all.

One Day at a Time

by Steven Fuchsluger

Twelve years ago I began to experience a deepening of my love for Christ in the Eucharist. It began when I made a commitment to attend daily Mass once a week during Lent. It wasn't a practice that I had intended to continue beyond Lent, but when Easter came, I found that I didn't want to stop going to Mass. I discovered that my love for Christ had grown, my personal experience of his friendship had deepened, and my desire to spend more time with him in this way had increased.

In addition, daily Mass allowed me to grow in my knowledge and love of Christ through the priest's reflections on the readings in his homily. The rich truths of the faith that were unpacked during those few minutes were a great treasure. Today, I attend daily Mass whenever my job schedule and family duties allow.

Then, about five years ago, I began to visit Christ in the Blessed Sacrament chapel for an hour every Sunday afternoon. Keeping my appointment with the Lord was a sacrifice at times, particularly when I had to leave in the middle of family activities or arrange for another person to take my place in the chapel. Even so, the incredible peace and closeness to Christ that I experienced in that hour-long visit were far greater than I ever could have hoped or imagined.

I continued to make my regular holy hour in adoration of our Lord on Sunday afternoons for about three years. Then my wife took my place at Sunday adoration, while I assumed the role of watching our wonderful children. Although I missed those extraordinary Sunday visits, it gave me great joy to know that my wife was enjoying that special time with Jesus. Currently, I spend my weekly hour with Christ on Wednesday mornings before I go to work.

The time I have spent with Christ at daily Mass and in Eucharistic adoration has been a source of comfort as well as a path to greater trust in my heavenly Father's tremendous love for me. The power of the Eucharist has changed my life. Thank you, God, for your great generosity!

From Adoration to Witness

by Maryella Hierholzer

Although I am a "cradle Catholic," I was raised in a mixed-faith background with many relatives who were Calvinists. Because the different views of Jesus held by the two groups confused me, I felt more comfortable as a child and even as a young adult just praying directly to God the Father or to the Holy Spirit. To me Jesus seemed judgmental, demanding, and unforgiving. I always received the Eucharist, but if I needed help I was more likely to ask Mary to intercede with her son for me than I was to go to Jesus directly.

That prayer practice started to change two years ago, when I became very ill in a foreign country, far away from my home and family. I had very little support in my illness and spent many hours alone. I heard an American nun speaking on a British radio station. I smirked that this was the Mother Angelica in Alabama that my own earthly mother had encouraged me to listen to for nearly twenty years. So I listened to Mother Angelica again. Gradually I began to know that Jesus Christ is really with me and is someone I can talk to.

I moved back to the United States and started tuning into EWTN in the evenings, when I was still weak from the remnants of my illness. I found that there was a regular program every Saturday night featuring a convert to Catholicism and a person who had left the faith and later returned to it, who talked about the church and the Bible. I started reading the Bible and found not only Jesus on every page but also the

Catholic Church. I am still in awe at everything our Lord and loving God has left us.

I registered at St. Louis Catholic Church in Clarksville, Maryland, and noticed that they had given me a form during registration to sign up to help with parish activities. There was a box to check for adoration of the Blessed Sacrament. I felt drawn to it and checked the box. Soon I was scheduled to come for an hour each Sunday. I also started attending the Marian devotion at the Shrine of St. Anthony the first Sunday of every month, during which the Blessed Sacrament is also exposed.

It's been about nine months now since I checked that box. There are no events during my week that fill me with greater joy than adoration of the Blessed Sacrament. It's during that one hour each Sunday that I can really feel comfortable talking directly to Jesus. My life has changed and so have the lives of others. I started to notice that I was being called to talk to non-Catholic Christians and nonbelievers about the Catholic Church. I have never felt the Holy Spirit act so strongly in me before.

Last October I traveled on a business trip with a Protestant-turned-Buddhist co-worker who seemed to have a negative opinion of Catholicism. The first evening of the trip he complained that he had nothing to read and asked what I had brought with me. I replied that I had a book about the early church fathers and the Mass, but that I was certain that he wouldn't want to read it! He replied that in fact he really did want to read the book. I was stunned. I gave him the book, and every morning at breakfast we talked about Jesus. He noted that he had never seen Jesus presented like he had in this particular book.

That was the Holy Spirit working! I was merely a carrier of Christ's message. But the fact that I was reading that book and had the courage to talk about Jesus and his church were a result of the many hours I spent at adoration and benediction.

It is still hard for me to pray directly to Jesus when I am not in the presence of the Blessed Sacrament. But Jesus understands, and we're getting there together. At adoration, I hear his encouragement to talk to people about the Catholic Church and bring them home to him. I have two job credentials for this work: I know what it's like to have non-Catholic relatives, and I know how hard it can be to pray to Jesus after his image has been so marred in the past few hundred years.

Jesus, I believe I know why you gave us the Eucharist before you died. With so many different opinions and forms of worship in the world, you knew that it would become difficult for many of us to pray to you. Thank you, Lord, for giving us your simple presence in the Eucharist, free from people's judgments and interpretations.

Procession of Love

by Jennifer Schuberth

Imagine a darkened gym full of teens and young adults sitting on the floor in anticipation. In the center of the gym, present among us for the entire weekend, has been a candle tower, which holds the glorious monstrance. This candle tower and the exposed Eucharistic Jesus have been there in the center of everything. Jesus has been there with us, changing hearts, quietly calling to us.

Saturday night it begins. A seminarian lifts the monstrance high from the candle tower and begins the procession, weaving slowly through the crowd. All fall on their knees. In this darkened room, our precious, illuminated Jesus provides the light!

Believers and unbelievers, those who are troubled and those who are at peace, those who question and those whose faith is already somewhat strong, people from all walks of life—all lift their eyes and hearts to Jesus in the Eucharist. He is so compelling.

We are encouraged to reach out and touch the cloak that is used to hold the monstrance as the procession goes by. Jesus seems to be saying to all, "Just ask me. Open your heart and soul to me. I want to change your life! I want to heal you and bring you closer to me."

As he draws near, we surrender. Silently, we cry, we petition, we talk to our Lord with all our hearts. His love is so powerful and so present! His peace is pervasive. We reach out and touch the cloak that holds the monstrance. We want to be as close as we can to Jesus.

The procession moves on. We turn to follow him. Our hearts yearn for him. We follow with our eyes, our hearts, and our prayers. Our senses are all focused on him. Never before have we felt so united with him. We pour out our hearts. We love.

One silently prays, "Use me Lord." Another prays, "Move my heart, Jesus. Make me your own." Still another cries out to Jesus, "I am so sorry, Lord. Help me." Yet another pours out, "I love you, Lord. I love you so much." Still another prays from the heart, "I have been lost without you, Jesus. Show me the way."

The room is filled with the Holy Spirit, prayers, incense, and soft music. You can feel the love. You can feel the Lord's presence. You know he is reaching out to you as you reach out to him. Hearts are healed. Souls turn back to him, straightening their paths in life. We all seek the one who is love.

In time, the procession must end. The Eucharist is put back at the top of the candle tower for adoration. Through the night, we are allowed to quietly come back and pray to our precious Jesus.

Every year, the seminarians at Mount St. Mary's University offer this tremendous gift of a Eucharist-centered weekend to teens and young adults at "Mount 2000 and Beyond." I have brought groups for many years, because I wanted more young people to experience what my children and I have discovered—the transforming, powerful peace to be had from spending a weekend with Jesus in the Eucharist.

Questions for Reflection

1. What dispositions of the heart do you think opened the writers in this chapter to Jesus' power and presence during Eucharistic adoration?

2. How often are you able to spend time with Jesus in Eucharistic adoration? What has been your own experience when you do so?

3. In his encyclical on the Eucharist, the late Pope John Paul II said that "Christians must be distinguished above all by the 'art of prayer'" and encouraged the faithful to worship the Eucharist outside of Mass. In what ways would you like to grow in your prayer life? How would regular adoration of the Eucharist help?

CHAPTER 5

Eucharistic Ministry

Do not, therefore, regard the bread and wine as simply that, for they are, according to the Master's declaration, the body and blood of Christ. Even though the sense suggests to you the other, let faith make you firm. Do not judge this matter by taste, but be fully assured by faith, not doubting that you have been deemed worthy of the body and blood of Christ.

—St. Cyril of Jerusalem

The Big Shout

by Jacki Holecek

When planning for any journey, it's always wise to prepare for the unexpected. I think that this is especially true when I reflect on my spiritual journey with the Eucharist. When I was preparing for my first Communion in 1955, little did I realize where the journey was going to take me and what unexpected joys I would receive along the way.

It was with great anticipation that I prepared for receiving my Lord for the first time. I must admit that as a seven-year-old I might not have had a complete grasp of the meaning of the Eucharist, and I was also caught up with the trappings of having a first Communion party and the fact that I was going to receive presents. Yet I believe that on some level I truly did understand that the most important gift I received from the Eucharist was God's grace.

On my spiritual journey, my faith and love for Jesus and the Eucharist continued and were nurtured by my mother, by the sisters at school, and by the parish priests. All through my life with all of its challenges, the gift of God's grace in the Eucharist has sustained me. I am so very thankful for the Lord's presence in my life and for the people who have helped me on my journey.

Throughout my life I have felt a need to enrich and deepen my relationship with the Lord through prayer and the reception of Jesus in the Eucharist. I have learned that we need to listen when the Lord is speaking to us. And I have also learned that when the Lord wants us for something, he won't let go until we do what he wants.

I had such an experience in 1995. The Lord's voice started out as a whisper, but it grew into a big shout! A friend had been trying to convince me to become an extraordinary minister of Holy Communion. Like many, I felt that I was unworthy to perform in this role. But because of my relationship with the Lord and my trust in him, I was willing to give it some consideration. Then came the Lord's "big shout"! Until this time our parish had distributed the body and blood of Christ only under the form of the host. But a decision had been made to distribute the Eucharist under both species—bread and wine—and to accomplish this, they were going to need more ministers. Our pastor announced that there was going to be a training class for new ministers and asked for volunteers to meet him after Mass. As I prepared to leave the church, I still wasn't sure that this ministry was right for me. But when I saw the pastor holding up a sign that said, "All Sinners Welcome to Join," I knew that the Lord was addressing me. Like many others, I may have been unworthy, but the Lord wanted me anyway.

I had always had a great love for the Eucharist. After I became a Eucharistic minister, that love became more intense than I ever could have imagined. Before, it had been about me and my needs, my relationship, my love for the Lord. Now, it is about sharing Christ's body and blood with others and trying to bring the love I feel for the Lord and the Eucharist to everyone. The love that the Eucharist inspires in me is so tremendous that I feel compelled to share it with everyone. I now pray constantly for those people who do not know the

Lord and do not receive him in the Blessed Sacrament, and I try to extend an invitation to all to join us at Mass and see what they are missing.

Back in 1955 I couldn't have imagined that my journey was going to lead me to a point where I would be overwhelmed by the desire to bring the Blessed Sacrament to the most precious person in my life. This person had been estranged from the church and the sacraments for a very long time. Our Lord is always with us, and through my relationship with him he knew that my greatest need was to see this person be reconciled with him. I thank the Lord for hearing my prayer and thank my pastor for responding to this call.

I'm not sure where the rest of the journey will lead me, but I'll be ready when the Lord calls. Lord, I am not worthy to receive you. Thank you for saying the word and healing me so that I can serve you and others!

A Gift of Love

by Christina Delaney

My friend Susan had been going through a rough year. Not only had she undergone cancer surgery, but she spent nearly all of her time caring for her mother, Elisabeth, who was in her tenth year of suffering from Alzheimer's disease. I had moved to Maryland only a few years before, and soon became involved with people and ministries at Our Lady of the Fields Church. That's where I met Susan. At first, we didn't seem to have very much in common. Although we both have three children, hers were grown and mine were still in school. She grew up in this area and had many friends and family members nearby. My family members lived quite a distance away, and I was in the process of making new friends. Yet somehow we felt drawn to each other in spirit, because we shared the same great love for our Lord, Jesus Christ.

I had just become a Eucharistic minister for the residents of the Annapolitan Nursing Home in Arnold, Maryland. I truly enjoyed serving them, and each time I carried my pyx containing the body of Christ from Mass to the nursing home, I felt a surge of joy and excitement. Bringing Jesus to those who could not come to him was a humbling experience. Shortly after I began this ministry, I had an idea of how I might be able to help Susan.

Elisabeth was growing very weak, and Susan hadn't been able to go to daily Mass recently because she stayed by her mother's side day and night. So I called Susan and offered to bring the Eucharist to them the next day. She eagerly accepted and gave me directions to her mother's house. I looked forward to meeting her mother, because I had heard so much about her. But since I didn't know what her physical condition was, I wasn't sure that she would be able to consume an entire host. So, I brought only one host, thinking that I could break off a small piece to give to Elisabeth.

Susan greeted me when I arrived, and when I walked into the living room, I saw Elisabeth in her bed and several other people in a back room. There seemed to be a bit of commotion, but when they saw me enter the room, everyone quieted down and allowed me to proceed with prayer and a Scripture reading. When it came time to distribute Communion, I thought that I would have to break the host into many small pieces to accommodate everyone who was present. But only Susan and her husband, Bill, asked to receive the Eucharist. I couldn't tell if Elisabeth was aware of her surroundings; I could see, however, that she would not be able to consume even a small piece of the host, since she had lost the ability to swallow.

I gave half of the host to Susan and the other half to Bill. Then, the most beautiful thing happened. Before Susan put the host into her mouth, she touched it to her mother's lips and said, "Here, Mom, receive Jesus." What a loving gesture! And what a precious gift for a daughter to give her mother. When Susan was a child, Elisabeth gave her daughter nourishment. Now, Susan was able to give spiritual food to her mother with such a loving gesture!

Nearly an hour later, after I had returned home, I received a phone call: Shortly after I had left Elisabeth's home, she died. I felt God's presence so powerfully at that moment that I almost dropped the phone. Elisabeth was waiting for Jesus to come to her in the Eucharist before she went to meet him face-to-face. She was at peace, and I felt a sense of awe at having been the feet to bring our Lord to a loving daughter to give to her dying mother.

More Precious Than Diamonds

by Nancy Baker

It had not been a good day. It began with the blue flashing lights of the officer's motorcycle. I was late going to the hospital where I distribute Communion to the patients. My mind was racing ahead of me, trying to compensate for the fact that I overslept that morning. I was truly shocked to realize that I had been speeding. The officer was unfailingly polite as he handed me my ticket, but I gritted my teeth when he wished me a nice day. "Nice day, my foot. You've already ruined it," I thought, as I insincerely smiled back at him. Then I railed at God: "How could you let this happen? I'm going to do *your* work!" But I knew in my heart that it wasn't God's fault that I got a ticket. I was the one who had been speeding.

I was not in a pleasant mood when I arrived at the hospital. And I certainly wasn't in the proper frame of mind to take our Lord present in the Eucharist to his sick and hurting people. As I hurried to the chaplain's office, I was determined to get this hospital visit over with quickly. I was stunned to find thirty-eight names on the list of patients to be seen. Normally, there were about twenty. So much for getting finished quickly!

I went to the chapel and asked God to give me his grace to change my attitude. I believe that outwardly I did manage to appear compassionate, but inwardly I was still resentful—sort of like I was when I got the speeding ticket a few minutes earlier. Even so, I know that the Lord uses us in spite of our failings. And even if I didn't *feel* loving while I was doing it, I was still ministering to his people.

Three hours later, I was finally down to my last patient. I encountered a big red stop sign on his door. Upon inquiring at the nurse's station, I learned that the patient had tuberculosis and that a mask was required to enter the room. I struggled with the contraption. The elastic pulled at my ears. My glasses fogged up when I breathed. And being a bit claustrophobic, I was more than a little uncomfortable.

As I was about to enter the room, a nurse touched my shoulder. "He speaks no English," she informed me. "Oh, great!" I thought. Just what I needed. I dragged out my Spanish translation and prepared to use a lot of hand gestures. But once I was inside the room, a slight Hispanic man peered at me with questioning eyes. A touch of real compassion surged though me. How frightening it must be to have a serious disease and not be able to communicate. It took a lot of gesturing before he understood why I was there. When I showed him the Consecrated host, recognition flashed in his eyes. "Sí, Sí!" he exclaimed.

I was very conscious of the fact that there was TB in the man's room, and I didn't want to touch anything—or him, for that matter. I had planned to place the host in his hand, but after I stumbled through the Spanish version of the Communion rite, I was surprised to see him close his eyes and open his mouth. Just as I leaned over to place the body of Christ on his tongue, he turned his head to cough. Given the fact that he had TB, I was glad that he turned his head, but unfortunately I had already let go of the host. Where it fell was anybody's guess. I searched; he searched. I motioned for him to shake out his bedding. I checked the floor and the crevices of the bed. Then I panicked. I had lost our Lord—*lost him!* I had an inkling of how our Blessed Mother felt when she realized that Jesus was missing from the caravan after their visit to Jerusalem. No amount of probing produced the host.

Finally, I gave him another host and resolved to find the chaplain to see what to do. Never in all my years as a Eucharistic minister had this happened to me. As I was leaving the room, I jerked my mask off, releasing some of my frustration. Head down, tears threatening, I started to seek out Fr. John. I reached up to tug at my ear, as is my habit when I'm deep in thought, and I realized that one of my small diamond earrings was missing. "Oh, no," I thought. "What else could go wrong?"

I examined the hallway just outside the room. A kind nurse asked me what the problem was and even helped me search, but to no avail. "Perhaps, it's in the room," she suggested. "Let me check for you." She expertly whipped on a mask and disappeared behind the red stop sign. I know she must have searched thoroughly, because the wait seemed like forever.

She was a devout Catholic, I learned as she came out of the room. "I'm so sorry, I didn't find your earring," she said in hushed tones. "But I found something more precious than diamonds." Into my hands she very gently laid the consecrated host, which she had carefully wrapped in a clean white handkerchief.

The whole day clicked into perspective then. Yes, I had been doing the Lord's work, but I had lost sight of the pricelessness of our Lord present in the Eucharist. The Lord has given us this way to stay close to him, and I had been treating the

Eucharist as a product of my efforts. I was so humbled. I confessed my arrogance to him in the chapel. I thanked him that this day I did find something more precious than diamonds.

I never did find that earring. Sometimes people ask me why I wear only one earring when I am at the hospital. More often, they tell me I've lost an earring. "I know," I reply. I wear just one to remember that day and to remind me that neither gold, nor silver, nor diamonds could ever be as precious as our Lord present in the Eucharist.

Up Close and Personal

by Dolores Piligian

My first experience with being "up close and personal" with the Eucharist was the day I received my first Holy Communion. But even though I received the body of Christ into my mouth, I still felt somewhat removed from it. At that time only the priest was permitted to distribute Communion, and the sisters at our school taught us that we couldn't even let the host touch our teeth. I never dreamed that one day I would have the honor of distributing the Eucharist myself.

The opportunity came about ten years ago when I responded to an invitation in our church bulletin to join the hospital visitation ministry as a Eucharistic minister. Talk about being "up close and personal"—not only did I visit people in the hospital, I was able to bring the Holy Eucharist to comfort them. To go from not letting the host touch my teeth to actually being able to hold it in my hand and give it to someone else was an honor beyond my wildest dreams.

I have had so many wonderful visits with the people in the hospital. From the many heartfelt expressions of gratitude and the tears and the smiles we share, I know I made the right decision by saying yes to the invitation to become a Eucharistic minister. Not only do I feel that I help others by bringing the Eucharist to them, I also feel that I have benefited by becoming closer to the Holy Eucharist myself.

After I visit the last patient for the day, I spend some time in the hospital chapel praying for the people I have seen. The same feeling comes over me that I had after watching the movie *The Passion of the Christ*—Lord, I am not worthy. But I have been very blessed that, through the Eucharist, Jesus has allowed me to be "up close and personal" with him and to share the precious gift of his body and blood with those in need of his healing.

I Am with You Always

by Kathleen Schmidt

As I sat facing the stained-glass window depicting the ascension in my former parish in Long Island, New York, a question came to my mind that I had thought about before. What did Jesus mean when he said the words written under the scene, "Lo, I am with you always, even until the end of the world" (Matthew 28:20), as he began to ascend to heaven?

Since he left the earth and then in ten days sent the Holy Spirit to be with us, how could he be with us always?

It was quite a while later, when my husband and I began to travel to different time zones around the world, that I realized exactly how Jesus was with us always until the end of the world. It was in the Eucharist! While that would seem to be self-evident based on the words of Scripture and the liturgy, it did not become real to me until I understood that the holy sacrifice of the Mass is celebrated every day, all day long, all over the world. Jesus Christ's body, blood, soul, and divinity under the appearance of bread and wine is with us wherever the Blessed Sacrament is present.

After I had the privilege of becoming an extraordinary minister of Holy Communion, Jesus' presence in the Eucharist became even clearer to me. One Sunday I began to understand the great humility of our Creator. Through his Son Jesus Christ, in a small circle of bread, he was giving himself in love to all who approached to receive the Eucharist. Young and old, wealthy and poor, with rough or smooth hands, they received Jesus and returned to their seats. Tears filled my eyes as I watched my sisters and brothers in Christ walk away with him in their hearts—some knowing what and whom they held in their hearts and souls, and some, not. It didn't matter— Jesus gave himself in love to all who came to the table.

What unconditional love! That is the miracle of the Eucharist. I know now that I must follow my dear Lord's continued example in giving of myself humbly, unselfishly, and with unconditional love as he still does for us all day, every day, "twenty-four/seven."

The Teaching Hospital

by John Gregrich

Just how holy does a person have to be to serve as a Eucharistic minister? I used to think that Eucharistic ministers must be a cut above, possessing a deeper faith and a richer spiritual life than the rest of us. Then, about seven years ago, I became one myself. I didn't sense a calling to this particular ministry, but simply an awareness that my father, who died after a long illness, nearly a thousand miles away, had received the Eucharist frequently from the visiting clergy and laity of his parish. Realizing that there were ailing parents, with distant children, in my own community, I acted initially out of a sense of reciprocity. I continue now out of a sense of awe.

In my years as a Eucharistic minister, I have brought Communion to more than seven hundred people in the local public hospital—and to about a hundred of those more than once. Add to that the innumerable communicants who have received the host or cup from me when I have filled in at a Sunday or weekday Mass, and the total seems staggering to me. God has allowed me to share his presence with so many, yet I am not a pious man. I don't have the close personal relationship with my Lord and Savior, Jesus Christ, that some believers claim to have. Apparently I'm deficient in what Father Andrew Greeley calls "the Catholic imagination." I'm a concept guy who seeks to grasp the tenets of my faith intellectually—science and faith operate together in my mind. In this regard, I am most indebted to Einstein, for the simple elegance of $E = MC^2$, which shatters our feeble categories that separate energy from matter and offers an intellectual assist to our faith approach to the Real Presence.

Fortunately, the hospital is there to offer respite from such abstract thought. Intellectual assent is not even a component of my visits. Rather, these visits are concrete, personal, experiential, faith-saving events for me. In this setting, I am able to be Christ for others, despite my inability to claim him for myself. The hospital patients serve me as mentors. Their humility, humor, hospitality, dignity, and (of course) faith are striking. Regardless of how swollen, deformed, or discolored their bodies, no matter the degree of pain or uncertainty they are experiencing, they are not embarrassed by my presence. They are not self-conscious. They welcome me as the minister of the Eucharist they long for. They are eager to share a prayer, a tear, a worry, and often a chuckle. The gospel message of service as privilege is most palpable when I am learning from these faith-filled people.

Thanks to this ministry, my faith has become more concrete; but experience tells me that I'll be "on the road to Emmaus," like Cleopas in Luke's gospel (Luke 24:18), for a good long time. I only seem to really "get it" in the sharing of the bread. Fortunately, many are willing to show me the way and to share the bread with me, as well.

"My Lord and My God"

by Phyllis Y. Desbordes

Serving as a Eucharistic minister is a constant reminder as well as an outward manifestation of the very personal relationship that I feel Jesus allows me to have with him. I truly love the story of Lazarus (John 11:3-44), and I used to be envious of the beautiful friendship that Martha, Mary, and Lazarus enjoyed with Jesus. As I have matured in faith, I have come to understand that through the sacraments Jesus provides that same opportunity for each of us today to interact with him in a beautiful and personal way.

All of the sacraments were initiated by God as a way for us to communicate with him and to allow him into our lives, but in the Eucharist Jesus gives us his very self. At the Last Supper Jesus took bread, "and when he had given thanks he broke it and gave it to them, saying 'This is my body which is given for you'" (Luke 22:19). As a Catholic I was taught, and I truly believe, that when these words are repeated during the Mass, a transformation takes place. I acknowledge this transformation by tapping my heart lightly and saying, "My Lord and my God." Jesus also said to "do this in remembrance of me." Each time that I receive and distribute the Eucharist, I am reminded of his passion, death, and resurrection.

Participating in my ministry allows me to feel personally involved in carrying out the words spoken by Jesus as he shared bread and wine with the disciples prior to those events. For me the experience is as uplifting and rewarding as

I imagine his presence must have been for Martha, Mary, and Lazarus. When I consider that in my early years as a Catholic, only the priest was allowed to touch the host, I cannot imagine a greater privilege or blessing than being able to serve at the Lord's table today as an extraordinary minister of Holy Communion.

Life Choices

by Carlos Almeida

I attended Catholic schools all of my life—up to and including college at the Catholic University of America. I can remember every important Catholic rite of passage vividly, from my first Communion through my confirmation. Growing up, my heroes were my father (a physician), my mother (a teacher), and last but not least my parish priest. I can recall not being able to decide whether I should be a physician like my father, a teacher like my mother, a priest like my pastor, or an astronaut—doesn't every kid want to be one? To my regret, I never became an astronaut. And yet as a physician, a former teacher's aide, and a Eucharistic minister, I have in some way fulfilled the other three of my childhood dreams.

In college, I seriously considered the path to priesthood instead of medical school. However, I felt that God was directing me to help others through the healing arts, and I have never regretted my decision. I taught college biology for a while, but had difficulty relating to large groups of students. I concluded that I wasn't suited for teaching and that I could educate patients better as a physician than I ever could as a professor. Finally, I realized that my incredible fear of public speaking would hinder my ability to give homilies as a parish priest.

I love being a physician, and I think I would also have liked to be a priest. But the delight I experience giving the Eucharist to my fellow parishioners is more rewarding than educating my patients about their ailments, and is almost as satisfying as being a tool of God's healing grace for my sick and dying patients.

But the greatest reward for me in becoming a Eucharistic minister is the ability it gives me to encourage my youngest son to accept and enjoy the special gift of our Lord Jesus Christ in the Eucharist. He was excited about his first Communion but was reluctant to receive our Lord after that first experience. Yet when I serve as minister of the host, he is willing to receive from me, and has come to learn how special Communion can be. I look forward to someday being able to provide this privileged service to believers who are ill and are in the hospital, as well.

I believe that all through my life God has guided my experiences and my choices. I am grateful to have had an opportunity to try teaching, to be able to relieve suffering as a physician, and most of all, to have an opportunity to share the great gift of the Eucharist with my son and with others. For everything he has done for me, thanks be to God!

Questions for Reflection

1. In these stories, how was the presence of Christ manifested in the Eucharistic ministers? How did their personal presence help those to whom they were bringing the Eucharist?

2. We can be tempted to decline serving in a ministry, whether as a Eucharistic minister or in some other capacity, because we feel unworthy to do so. Why is this feeling of unworthiness based on a false premise? What can you do to combat this temptation?

3. Reflect on ways that you have served God's people in the past. In what ways do you think he might be calling you to serve now?

CHAPTER 6

The Body of Christ

Jesus Christ gives himself entirely to us; he unites his sacred body with ours; and, by this union, we become one and the same spirit with him. As the food which we take nourishes our body, so the Holy Eucharist is the nourishment of our soul. For even as our bodily food is changed into our substance, so the Holy Eucharist transforms us into Jesus Christ.

—St. John Baptist de la Salle

"Dazzled"

by Brenda Rathgeb

Do I love the Eucharist? For years, I have been praying to be "dazzled" by this sacrament. I hear people speak of having mystical experiences at Mass, and I want to have them, too. But I am Thomas—doubting, but praying, "My Lord and my God!" I am Mary Magdalene at the empty tomb, wondering where they have taken my Lord. I am the deer in Psalm 42, longing for the streams of living water.

What is the definition of "Eucharist"? Is it thanksgiving or healing? Is it "communion," as in the communion of saints, or the "body of Christ," as in the church? Or is it all of these?

I began to really look at the faces and situations of the people in my life—people that I am privileged to share Christ with in the ministry to the sick and homebound. To me, this is the Eucharist—the homebound old woman who loves me because "you bring me my Jesus." It is the residents of a nursing home, in varying stages of dementia, who may not even remember their own names, yet utter the familiar responses when praying those rote prayers and receiving the host in Communion. It is the young teenager with sickle-cell disease who is blind and paralyzed from a stroke but is always thrilled to receive the Eucharist and thank God for her blessings. It is the faith and the reverence of the woman who must be dressed and "brushed" to receive her God. It is the old couple, always seemingly at odds, who are praying for each other with such love from their sickbeds. It is my father, a very ordinary man with unwavering faith, who died peacefully and unafraid this past winter. And it is my five-year-old granddaughter, who in her innocence exclaimed, "This box that Granddaddy is in has handles so the angels can carry him right to Jesus."

When I reflect on these and all the other blessings in my life, I realize that, yes, I am "dazzled"—I truly do love the Eucharist.

A Sense of Connectedness

by Dee Matthews

My Catholic faith has always been a comfort to me. For many years, though—throughout my childhood and much of my adult life—I never really thought about why. As I have progressed in my faith journey and pursued opportunities to learn more about my beloved faith, I have become more aware of why I find it so fulfilling. I truly believe that the Eucharist is the "comfort food" that defines not just who I am, but who I am in relation to others.

My mother died when I was seven years old. I was devastated by the loss of her loving and caring presence but also by the loss of my sense of connectedness. I still can recall a very sad feeling of being alone and abandoned. Shortly after her death, another crisis arose. Quite understandably, my father was unable to find someone willing to care for me and for my five brothers and sisters while he was at work. His only solution was to send us to St. Leo's Orphanage in Baltimore until we were older and able to stay at home by ourselves. Thus, I encountered another parental separation and another loss of my self-worth and sense of belonging.

While I was at St. Leo's, I attended St. Vincent's church and school. It was there in 1954 that I received my first Holy Communion. Inexplicably, within my small being I felt a connection; somehow, I felt attached, and I have continued to this day to feel that attachment every time I receive the Lord in Communion. Of course, at the time I couldn't articulate this feeling, but I knew in my heart that I belonged to and was a part of something wonderful.

Although people didn't talk about the connection between church and the family in the fifties, I felt that I was part of a much bigger whole; it was a warm and welcoming family-type feeling. The concept of church as family did not need to be defined in order for me to experience it.

In a book I read by Mary Ann Fatula, *The Triune God of Christian Faith*, this concept is explained very well:

> We know by experience how much we have the need to belong to a family of some kind. But this need is ours because we have come from a God who is not an isolated monad but a tri-personal community of love. The divine persons are unreserved self-giving; they hold back nothing of themselves for themselves. All that the Father, Son, and Spirit are, they pour out on one another without reserve. But through the paschal mystery of Jesus they pour themselves out upon *us* also without reserve.

And since we are all in communion with each other, I can actually feel that family bond when I receive the Eucharist. I can identify with Christ because he is also human. Through his life, death, and resurrection, I feel joined to him and to our church family of believers as a sister, and I know that his loving Father is also my loving Father.

During the consecration of the bread and wine at Mass, I have a rich, vibrant image of our heavenly Father in resplendent glory. He appears as our patriarch with wisdom, kindness, justice, and love in his eyes as he looks upon us in fellowship with Christ. Jesus is the God-Man, who imbues the very essence of love and welcomes us to his banquet through the soundless whispering of the Holy Spirit. And we in procession, as brothers and sisters in faith, love, suffering, and joy, consume the precious gift of Christ himself. We are in total communion with each other, and I have a wonderful feeling of belonging. Now I can be Christ to all I meet.

But there is another thread to this story. As whole and as joined as I feel when I receive Christ at Mass, there is another way the Eucharist works in my life. This happens in the more private devotion of Eucharistic adoration. I am fed in a totally different way when I am lost in veneration of the Lord the first Friday of every month. I call this my retreat time—my time to be alone with Christ. This is when Christ and I have our cozy conversations. This is when I listen to the Lord and he listens to me. This is the time I pour out all my fears, joys, angers, longings, and frustrations. This is where I bring him my most fervent prayers for my family, my friends, and my loved ones who have gone to their reward. This is where, though exhausted, I am refreshed, and though alone, I am not lonely.

I am a catechist in our confirmation program at Our Lady of Grace in Parkton, Maryland. One of the most important tenets that I strive to pass on to our *confirmandi* is that without the Eucharist in our lives, it is very difficult to be the priest, prophet, and king that we are called to be by our baptism and by the seal of confirmation. I hope they are listening!

United by the Blood of Jesus

by Jim Prosser

After having nuns for teachers in elementary school followed by eight years of Jesuit education, I imagine that I have always believed to some extent in the real presence of the Eucharist. Perhaps I just needed a little help with my unbelief.

Several years ago, in my late forties, I started to experience a significant spiritual awakening. A dramatic change, or *metanoia*, was taking place in my life goals and values. With this change, my appreciation of Jesus' gift of himself to us in the Eucharist has blossomed. I had learned in elementary school that my body is a temple of the Holy Spirit and that Jesus is always within us in a spiritual way. Gradually I began to understand that, through the Eucharist, Jesus is with us in a physical way as well.

We've often heard the church described as the body of Christ, where each one of us makes up a distinct and unique part of that body. On reflection, I realize that all Catholics in the body are not only spiritually related through the Eucharist, but that we also share Jesus' blood. After sharing many Communions together, we could be closer to each other than to the "blood brothers" that we may have bonded with in our youth.

Though our human nature is full of flaws, Jesus continuously offers us the opportunity to receive his love, his life, his strength, and his peace when we receive his body and blood. After I received Communion at the Holy Thursday Mass, I took a little time to think of all the people that had received the Eucharist in that same church over the last hundred years. It made me feel closer to those in the pews around me, even though I may have never met some of them before. Then I thought of how many people around the world receive the Eucharist every day and how many people throughout the ages are united to one another and to us through the gift of Christ's body and blood. Through the Eucharist, Christ is part of us, as we all are also one family as members of his body.

Next to his sacrifice at the crucifixion, the Eucharist—his own body and blood—is the most important gift that Jesus gave us. The Eucharist provides us with the graces that we need to be the evangelizers that Jesus commanded us to be. All we need to do to receive these graces is to fully believe in the Eucharist; to prepare for Mass spiritually, mentally, and physically; to receive the Eucharist reverently; and, afterwards, to reflect with Jesus quietly. When I can, I try to stay in my pew for a few minutes after Mass, to have a more personal reflection time with the Lord.

So many of us who have been Catholics from birth tend to take incredible beliefs for granted. It is not that we don't believe, but maybe that we don't believe as fully and as personally as we should. With Jesus as your partner, may your beliefs continue to strengthen. As the father of the possessed boy cried out to Jesus, "I believe; help my unbelief!" (Mark 9:24).

In Communion with Saints

by Howell A. McConnell

Some years ago, I attended a funeral Mass for a young woman who had died tragically from a brain tumor at the age of eighteen. Fr. Orr, of the Georgetown Preparatory School, gave a deeply touching homily. It was lyrical and inspired by his own experience of the deaths of his father and brother the previous year. During the consecration, I became gently aware of the host of saints in heaven coming to greet the young woman with great rejoicing. This was the first time that I had experienced the truth expressed in the new *Catechism* that at such a Mass we are in special communion with the deceased. After Mass, I shared my experience with several people who said that they had also had similar experiences.

Questions for Reflection

1. When we receive the Eucharist, we are united more closely to Christ, who unites us to all the faithful in one body. How does attending Sunday Mass or praying with your family help to make you aware of this unity? Reflect on other situations where you have experienced the unity of the body in Christ.

2. In his apostolic letter for the Year of the Eucharist, Pope John Paul II observed that in the celebration of the Eucharist, the church renews its "awareness of being a 'sign and instrument' not only of intimate union with God but also of the unity of the whole human race." How does our participation in the Eucharist give us a responsibility to care for other people in the world? In what ways might the Lord be calling you to carry out that responsibility?

3. Is there anyone in the body of Christ with whom you are experiencing a wounded or broken relationship? Is there anything you can do to repair the relationship? How would prayer for reconciliation help?

CHAPTER 7

Forgiveness and Healing

Of course you are unworthy. But
when do you hope to be worthy? . . .
All the good works that we could ever
do would never make us worthy, in
this sense, of Holy Communion. God
alone is worthy of himself, he alone
can make us worthy of him, and he
alone can make us worthy with his
own worthiness.

—St. Catherine of Siena

The Power to Heal

by Richard Ciamarra

I recently suffered through a "mystery" illness. Thirty-seven doctors examined me, and I stayed in the hospital five times, but no one could figure out what was wrong. However, I did get well—and I attribute my recovery to the power of the Holy Spirit along with the perseverance and devoted love of my wife, the faith and understanding of my mother-in-law, and my longing to receive the Eucharist again with my wife.

In October 2003 I began experiencing severe abdominal pain coupled with mental confusion. One moment I would be speaking normally with someone, and the next, I would be babbling incoherently. I truly thought that I was losing my mind.

My wife, Maureen, is a nurse and, I might add, a wife who wouldn't give up on the idea that something was truly wrong with her husband. One evening when all other avenues seemed to have been exhausted, Maureen decided to search the Internet after I had gone to bed. She had my medical records at her side, plus one thing the doctors didn't have or ever think of using—God. With confidence she called on the Holy Spirit to help her solve my problem.

After four hours spent pouring over my symptoms, my lab work, and the records of my hospital stays, she finally hit on something that made sense to her. The next day she went to her boss, the surgeon who had operated on me, and asked him to order a parathyroid test. She was in the room when the test was performed, and she actually saw the nodule on my right parathyroid. It was discovered through her perseverance and—she and I both believe—through the power of the Holy Spirit. Despite the previous months of frustration and disappointment, Maureen had a feeling on that particular night that something wonderful was aiding her search. The reason she asked for the test was that she noticed a small increase in the calcium level of my blood, which can be a sign of a parathyroid tumor. A few days later the benign tumor was removed. That was the end of problem number one—the confusion and incoherency disappeared. Unfortunately, however, the pain remained.

One joy that Maureen and I shared as a married couple was receiving the Eucharist together at Mass. Attending Mass had become difficult for me, though, because the pain was so great that I couldn't sit in one place for very long. With much persuasion, Maureen got me to church on Christmas Eve. I stood in the back of the church while Maureen and her mom sat in a pew up front. I was in terrible pain, but I prayed to God to give me the strength to stay through the Mass. I focused on the thought of our being at Mass together, and somehow I was able to get through it. I found out later that my pastor, who was in Rome attending Mass with the Holy Father, had offered the Christmas Eve Mass there for me.

On New Year's Eve the pain had become even worse, and again my wife called on the Holy Spirit for help. That afternoon, when most doctors' offices were already closed, she found a pain-management doctor and explained my problem. He asked her to bring me in. The doctor worked with me for four hours and said that he thought he had discovered my problem. He inserted twenty-seven syringes of an anesthetic solution into my abdomen and told me that if the pain stayed away for six hours, he would know how to treat me. The pain was gone for six hours, and so two days later he inserted thirty-two syringes of alcohol to kill the nerve endings that were causing the pain. By the end of February, I had improved remarkably and was able to deal with my pain.

I feel very blessed to have such an extraordinary wife, a wonderful mother-in-law, a supportive family, great friends, and God's grace and love to get me through this trying time. To be able to get back to church, share in the celebration of the Eucharist, and just hold hands with my wife during the Our Father are truly gifts from the Lord.

Thank you, Maureen, my love. And thank you, everyone who hung in there with me. Again, thank you, dear God. I know that because of this terrible experience, I have shared in Jesus' suffering, grown in faith, and become a better person.

A Loving and Forgiving God

Anonymous

Where do I begin to tell about the most powerful experience I have had before the Eucharist? My story starts in the late 1970s, when as an unmarried teenager, I became pregnant. In a time of doubt, fear, and confusion, I committed a sin that I will regret as long as I live—I aborted my unborn child.

About twenty years later I attended a Bible study designed for women who had undergone abortions, and through it I began to experience healing. But even then, I sometimes felt that God just couldn't forgive me—that I had committed a sin that was too big and too serious to ever be forgiven. I am sure Satan used that doubt to keep me questioning the awesome mercy of God.

Then came the time when God called me to his church. I began to attend RCIA classes, and I especially loved going to Eucharistic adoration. Before work one crisp November morning, I stopped at a one-hundred-year-old church in downtown Baltimore. I sat there with the sun streaming through the beautiful stained-glass windows, simply enjoying being in the presence of our Lord.

I had prayed to the Lord about my aborted child many times before. Was it a boy or a girl, I wondered? I had learned that naming a child who was aborted is an important step of the healing process.

As I prayed for God's forgiveness again, I suddenly had the feeling that I was not alone. I called God's name and asked, "Is that you?" His answer was, "Yes." At that moment, a shimmering, white being came down and sat beside me. For about the next fifteen minutes, he and I sat in each other's presence. From him I sensed no anger or condemnation, simply warm, unconditional love and joy.

Then the being left my side and went away. I was left feeling completely awestruck. What had I just experienced? When I told a devout friend about what happened, she believed (as I did) that I had received a great gift from God. He allowed me to feel his complete and total forgiveness for my sin from so long ago. I now felt that God was encouraging me to continue my RCIA preparation so I could enter the church at the Easter Vigil. What a blessing to receive the Sacraments of Reconciliation and the Eucharist, to have God always present with me.

Because of that November morning in adoration, I have a tangible sign from God himself that I am completely forgiven. Satan and his lies no longer have a hold on me! Like the psalmist says, "as far as the east is from the west," my sin has been removed from me (Psalm 103:12).

Do I love the Eucharist? *Absolutely!* I have no words to truly express the peace and joy it has brought to my life.

Saving Marriage at Mass

by Douglas and Annette Tinder

The power of Christ's presence in the Eucharist is certainly evident in our lives. In fact, it even saved our marriage.

We had only been married for five years, but we knew that our marriage was in trouble. Neither of us attended Mass on a regular basis. We were seeing a marriage counselor and attempting to work out our problems, yet still we felt that something was missing.

We knew in our hearts that if we went back to church together, our faith would become stronger, and our marriage would have a better chance of surviving. But since we weren't affiliated with a particular parish, the only question was, where? After much deliberation and procrastination, we decided to find the priest who met with us during our marriage preparation classes. We had really liked him because he was compassionate and open minded, and we were both confident that he would be able to help us.

Having been away from church for such a long time, it took a lot of willpower for us to go to Mass that spring morning. We hoped that the priest who had prepared us for marriage would be the celebrant, but we got more than we could ever have wished for. The atmosphere in the church was festive that Sunday, because as we soon learned, the congregation was celebrating Father's homecoming from sabbatical. This would be the first Mass he celebrated in his parish upon returning! In his homily, Father talked about the reasons he needed time away and told a story from the Bible that directly related to the problems we were having in our marriage.

After all these years, we can't remember the story he told, but we will never forget the significance of our coming to Mass that particular day. We believe that the Holy Spirit guided us to attend Mass on the day of Father's return. We had no idea that this was his first Mass since arriving home; moreover, everything he said applied to our marital problems and to our desire to strengthen our spirituality. It was as if he knew that we were coming and wrote his homily specifically for us! As we gazed at the Eucharist during the consecration, we both felt at peace and somehow knew that we were going to make it through this trying time. As if God were giving us a sign from heaven, while we were kneeling in prayer after Communion, the sun began to shine through the stained-glass windows on what had started out as a cloudy day. We certainly felt the light and warmth of God's love in our hearts that day!

After Mass we thanked Father for sharing his story and told him how much it meant to us. We continued to attend Mass regularly. And we began seeing Father for spiritual guidance to help us work through our marital problems. We consider him a very dear friend. We soon moved away from that parish in Utica, New York, but we returned a few years later so that Father could baptize our son.

We truly believe that the power of the Eucharist saved our marriage, helped us deepen our spirituality, and made us better servants of our Lord. As we write these words, we are celebrating fifteen years of marriage. With God's continued presence in our lives, we look forward to celebrating many more.

God's Merciful Love

by Greg Douglas

Although I have been Catholic all my life, my love for the Eucharist wasn't born until my thirties and forties—long after my first Holy Communion. In the words of St. Augustine, "too late have I loved Thee." Not too late as in fatal or final, fortunately. But too late in a sorrowful, regrettable, penitential sense. For to love the Eucharist is to love God, and to love God is to believe in God, and to believe in God is to hope in God. But I did not always hope in God.

My journey back to God began out of despair. How did I get in that condition? I believe that the simple answer is sin. I began to sin at a young age. Petty, minor sins are the reality of nearly everyone's first reconciliation. It wasn't long before the grace of that sacrament was lost. I stopped going to reconciliation by the time I was in my early teens. Soon I was committing ever more grievous sins. I was an immature young person, drifting deeper and deeper into darkness. A feeling of anxiety began to grow in me.

What was the source of my fear? I think it was the knowledge, in the hidden recesses of my being, that by sinning we are separating ourselves from God. Separation from God is inherently lonely, but even worse, it is life threatening. And all of us are afraid when our lives are at risk. Our lives cannot be sustained without God. In our "dying," we begin to search for him. Now, in suffering and in truth, I began to pray and to hope in God. "Save me. Please, God. Save me."

Wasn't this the prayer of the prodigal son? We read in the gospel, "But when he came to himself he said, 'How many of my father's hired servants have bread enough and to spare, but I perish here with hunger!'" (Luke 15:17). The prodigal son, with hope in his father, turned away from his life of sin and made the journey home. He hoped only for the simplest gift of bread to eat. What he received must have been beyond his comprehension: "But while he was yet at a distance, his father saw him and had compassion, and ran and embraced him and kissed him" (15:20). The father then ordered a banquet in celebration of his son's return, "for this my son was dead, and is alive again; he was lost, and is found" (15:24).

Jesus taught that to be saved we must "repent, and believe in the gospel" (Mark 1:15). And so I began to turn away from my sins and toward God. The turning point came sometime in my early twenties. I went to the church of my youth in the middle of the day. The church was empty. I approached the altar where I had received my first Communion, knelt before the Blessed Sacrament, and prayed for God's help. I sensed then that God would never leave me, but at the time I hadn't made the connection to God's constant presence on earth in the Eucharist. My prayer was the ageless prayer of sinful human beings who yearn for God's love and mercy.

St. Thomas Aquinas once wrote, "Oh Sacred Banquet, in which Christ becomes our food, the memory of his passion is recalled, our minds are filled with grace, and a promise of future glory is given to us." Once we truly appreciate Jesus' real presence in the Eucharist, we can begin to grasp the incredible gift of love that we have been given. When we receive the Eucharist, we receive God in the simplest appearance of "bread" to eat. What we truly receive is beyond our comprehension. Like the father in the story of the prodigal son, God sees us "at a distance"—sinful, imperfect, undesirable. Yet, in his great mercy, he desires us and comes to us. In the Eucharist God nourishes us with his very life. Within the sacred banquet of the Eucharist is our Lord's real presence and loving embrace. I believe that if Jesus were here on earth in human form, he would embrace me physically—give me a hug—not for being perfect, but for simply turning away from sin and turning back to him. Jesus longs for all of us to return to him. He sacrificed his life on the cross and gave us his very self so that we could be reunited with his love. In the Eucharist God embraces all repentant sinners and draws all humankind ever closer to himself.

A Personal Invitation

by Mary Gioia

Like so many of my generation, I went to Communion every time I attended Mass, and I received the Sacrament of Reconciliation once or twice a year. I thought I was growing in my faith because I also occasionally attended Mass during the week.

One Saturday morning when I arrived at Mass, I heard a very distinct interior voice instructing me to go to confession before I received Jesus that day. Suddenly something I had put out of my mind for more than ten years came back to me. I hadn't confessed this sin, but it just didn't seem to be that big of a deal. After all, it happened before I had even gotten married. Anyway, today was Saturday, and I had plans to visit my in-laws in New Jersey later in the day. I wouldn't have time to come to the Sacrament of Reconciliation in the middle of the afternoon. Surely, this was a case of my imagination working overtime. Still, what if this was an actual message from God?

I needed confirmation that God was speaking to me, and I needed it now. I asked for a sign. I had to think of something fast; we were now at the Liturgy of the Word. I needed to make my decision soon. I decided to ask God for a sign—for the priest to drop the host during the consecration. That had to be something out of the ordinary; I had never seen a priest drop the host at this solemn part of the Mass. If Father dropped the host, I thought, I would know that the message was from God.

Not only did the host slip out of the priest's hands at the consecration, it actually became airborne—as if some unseen hand had pulled it from the priest and flipped it in the air. Father managed to catch it just before it landed on the altar.

Needless to say, I was quite shaken. Now I knew that not only did I need to confess my sin, but that God had spoken directly to me in an effort to break down the wall that was separating me from him. In order to be a tabernacle of his presence in the Eucharist, I needed to receive his grace and mercy in the Sacrament of Reconciliation.

I didn't receive Communion that morning, and after Mass I went to confession in the sanctuary. I simply asked Father if he would hear my confession because I would be traveling later that day and wouldn't be able to come during the scheduled time. Ordinarily I would have been embarrassed to confess my sins face-to-face, but I felt God's generous graces supporting me.

I received Jesus' life-giving grace in the Sacrament of Reconciliation that morning, and the following day I received his body and blood in Holy Communion. What a blessed experience it was to be reunited to Jesus after such a personal invitation.

I was the woman at the well, whose entire life had been laid before her by our Lord. But unlike the woman at the well, I initially spoke of my experience only to my husband. I was afraid of what I would say if people asked me what I had confessed.

Now I realize that we are all sinners and that we need to admit it. We do more damage to our souls when we pretend that we have no need for the Sacrament of Reconciliation, because we separate ourselves from the Lord, who is longing to embrace us with his love and forgiveness. Jesus is eagerly waiting for us to come to him. We only need to accept his invitation.

Now I make it a practice to receive the Sacrament of Reconciliation at least once a month. I look forward to feeling the peace that comes from knowing that my sins have been wiped away and that I have been reunited to Christ. And I never again want anything to stand in the way of my receiving our blessed Lord.

Peace for Dying, Peace for Living

by Robert Wagner

"You have a cancerous growth on your kidney and pneumonia, which may indicate that the cancer has spread to your lungs." To a self-absorbed person like me, these words sounded like a death sentence. My first reaction was anger at the doctor for mistreating the symptoms, and then at God for letting this happen to me. God had been good to me all my life, and in my prayers I had promised many times that I would repay him in some way. But I always kept putting it off. After all, I was a young man. I could always do it later.

When I received my diagnosis of cancer at the age of fifty-eight, I figured that God had just gotten tired of waiting. I became completely obsessed with the idea of death. All the money and achievements that had meant so much to me no longer had any value. And I was afraid—not so much of dying, but of dying poorly; of not being able to handle the pain and suffering of death.

It was in this state of mind that I turned to my only possible salvation, the Eucharist. I went to St. Dominic's, the church of my first confession, my first Communion, and my wedding. I knelt and prayed to Jesus in the tabernacle. Nothing spectacular happened. But I started to feel at peace. The anger and resentment that had been consuming me began to slip away. I gave my heart and soul to the Lord, and in return he gave me peace.

That was seven years ago. The Lord not only gave me peace, he gave me back my life. I may have lost a kidney, but I didn't develop lung cancer. I don't know that I will ever be able to "repay" God for all he has done for me. But I do know that regardless of our failings, he is waiting and ready in the Eucharist to respond to our prayers if only we make the effort to come to him.

Questions for Reflection

1. What do you think is the relationship between forgiveness and healing? How can the Sacrament of Reconciliation, as preparation for reception of the Eucharist, help us to become aware of our need for healing?

2. What areas of your life—physical, spiritual, or emotional—may be in need of healing? When you receive Jesus in the Eucharist, how often do you remember to ask for healing?

3. In the parable of the prodigal son, with whom do you most identify—the son who went away and spent his father's inheritance, or the son who stayed with his father? Why were both sons in need of healing?

CHAPTER 8

Strength for the Journey

Lord, be the support of my weakness, you who have remained defenseless in the Eucharist so as to be the remedy for the weakness of your creatures.

—St. Josemaría Escrivá

Why Are You Afraid?

by George S. Brown

I had known Jesus in the Eucharist since my first Communion at St. Bernard Church in Waverly, Maryland, in 1932. I served as an altar boy at the Latin Mass many times in that church. I knelt with my younger brother Don for our hour of adoration during the Forty Hours devotion. I gazed at the host enclosed in the monstrance, convinced that Jesus was there reaching out to me, asking me to take strength in his presence. I assisted our priests in preparing incense for Benediction of the Blessed Sacrament. Along with the crowds that filled the church, I worshiped our Lord and God.

I repeated many of these same duties at the St. Charles College preparatory seminary, where for a short time I studied for the priesthood. I felt deeply the power and security Jesus gave me in the Eucharist. With Jesus' presence, I knew I had nothing to fear.

Yet, there would come a time when I felt truly afraid as I prepared to celebrate Mass.

Just before we sailed from California in January of 1944, the Navy assigned a Catholic chaplain to our 113th Naval Construction Battalion. I rejoiced that Fr. Howard E. Sammon had become a last-minute member of the Seabees. At our staging area in Finschhafen, New Guinea, I promptly returned to my acolyte duties, serving Fr. Sammon frequently at our battalion Masses.

From Finschhafen we moved into Hollandia, New Guinea,

an area that the Japanese had recently occupied. We spent a day chopping our way into the dense jungle, fighting the heat and the fierce red ants. I spent the first night with a machine-gun squad at an outpost, fearful of an enemy that might be within yards of our position.

Here Fr. Sammon and I were on the second day of our invasion into this war zone, preparing an altar for Mass on the hood of a Jeep. A small group of Seabees gathered around as we began, "*In nomine Patris, et Filii, et Spiritus Sancti.*" I don't know about the others, but I was terribly afraid until we reached those wonderful words, "*Hoc est enim corpus meum,*" "This is my body."

As Fr. Sammon held the host high above that unholy-looking Jeep, I gazed longingly and hopefully at Jesus. Then, I breathed a sigh of relief. I remembered the calming effect Jesus had on his disciples as he quieted the storm on the lake. Here he was in the Eucharist, calming a kid who feared an unknown enemy. For me, Jesus had come to my rescue. I knew that all would be well that day and in the days ahead. Jesus had been with me in the Eucharist for twelve years. I was certain he would walk with me for the rest of my life.

Our God Is Trustworthy

by Myra Welsh

As a Presbyterian child, I didn't have much of a grasp of what the Eucharist was for Catholics. But growing up in a

Catholic neighborhood, I gradually became aware of the Eucharist's significance. I remember one day when I was watching a group of boys play curb ball, one of them yelled, "Hi yah, Father," to a priest on the other side of the street. The priest didn't answer him. And when I asked the boy why, he explained, "Because Father is carrying Holy Communion to somebody." I turned and watched as the priest went silently on his way. I was dumbstruck by the silent reverence of that Catholic priest while he was carrying Communion.

But my most vivid memory is of a Christmas when my neighbor took me to her church to see the nativity scene. I have long since forgotten what the baby Jesus' crib looked like, but I can still see the burning candles and feel the warm air that flushed my cheeks as we opened the heavy door to the church. In the soft, golden light inside, I noticed a couple of the neighborhood roughnecks. I was surprised at how quiet they were but also that they piously genuflected and made the sign of the cross before they left the church. Somehow, I just knew that they were so reverent because Jesus was really *present* there.

Fourteen years later I married one of the neighborhood boys and spent the next five years reading about and studying the Catholic faith. Jesus didn't mince words when he said that he would give us his body to eat and his blood to drink, even though many walked away in disbelief. One day I just picked up the phone, called the rectory, and asked for instructions to become a Catholic. After months of prayer and study with Fr. Charles Meisel, I received the grace to believe and accept the teachings of the church. (May God reward the parish nuns who prayed for me.) I made my first Communion on Easter Sunday

1953 at St. Anthony of Padua Church in Gardenville. It was a wondrous, joy-filled time.

Yet just four years later, after the birth of my fourth child, I experienced postpartum depression and became angry with God that my life was so difficult. Like the Israelites in the desert, whose hardship quickly erased the memory of the parting of the waters and the manna from heaven, I forgot all of the blessings I had been given. I went to Mass weekly but didn't receive Communion, because I knew I would be lying if I told Jesus that I loved him. Oh, how merciful is our God, who patiently works with his children! I had not yet learned how to deal with angry emotions, how to speak honestly to my Father, and how to humbly ask for his help. Instead I let anger control my life. But even though I wasn't receiving Communion, Jesus was still interceding for me through his presence in the Eucharist. It took several months, but God's grace did its work, and I returned once again to the sacraments.

Seventeen faith-filled years went by. But again, life's circumstances turned stormy, complicated by surgery, three deaths in my family, a midlife crisis, and another depression. This trial was far more difficult to endure than the first, and though I fell briefly under the weight of this cross, by God's grace I was able to get back up. And this time, in addition to medical help, I turned to the Eucharist for support. We are not guaranteed an easy road in this life, but Jesus does promise to walk with us and to give us the grace that we need for each day. Oh, what comfort we forfeit and what misery we embrace, if we do not trust and turn to him!

I realized also that all the Bible verses I had memorized as a child and all the church teachings I had heard weren't enough by themselves: I had to integrate them into the core of my being. I had to learn the depths of humility and accept the fact that if I wanted to do God's will, I needed to ask for God's help, for I could not do it alone. I now thought I understood what Jesus meant when he said, "Take my yoke upon you" (Matthew 11:29). He would help me pull the load, no matter what road he led me down.

At Mass I began to offer all of my burdens to God alongside the bread and wine. By the power given to the priest by God, the bread became Christ's body, and the wine became his blood. I united myself with the prayer of the priest: "Through him, with him, and in him, in the unity of the Holy Spirit, all glory and honor is yours, almighty Father." I offered God my praise, gave thanksgiving for his mercies, asked for his forgiveness, and then placed all my petitions before our Father through his only Son, our mediator. Then, in Communion, Jesus came to embrace me, to nourish me, and to strengthen me for my journey. Although I didn't yet feel joyful emotions, I believed that God was giving me the strength to place one foot in front of the other for another week. This went on, year in and year out, for some years.

But our God is trustworthy, even giving patience for the journey. One day as I sat by my window looking out across the lawn at the Catholic church next door, I suddenly just knew: *I've made it!* Or, to be completely accurate, Jesus and I made it together! Tears of joy poured forth, soaking my cheeks and washing away the weary past.

Scripture tells us that Jesus longed to eat the Passover meal with his disciples the night before he suffered. Today, he still longs to share this meal with us—you and me—until he brings us safely home to our loving Father. I can truly witness that I live because Jesus lives in the Holy Eucharist. Alleluia! Amen.

Tiny in Size, Mighty in Power

by Mairzie Mulholland

"Middle age" is a term that rattles me a little. I can't pinpoint the precise moment when it crept into my vocabulary as a viable self-description, but it suddenly appeared and remains an unwelcome guest. With this term comes a multitude of imperfections that only age can forgive. Gravity and time take their toll on the body, as do a myriad of health concerns. You engage in familiar activities, but the body begins to respond in unfamiliar ways. With this in mind my doctor decided it was time to put me through a series of tests in order to rule out any major concerns. I was to enter the hospital as an outpatient, which is comforting only to the extent that I could plan on spending the night in my own bed. It also allowed me to attend morning Mass, which was a gift I was grateful to receive.

On this particular morning I was able to explain to Father before Mass that I had been fasting since the night before in order to undergo some tests. I wanted to receive Communion, but I was under strict orders from my doctor not to ingest anything but clear liquids. I was concerned that wine would not be a good idea on an empty stomach, so Father suggested that I take only the tiniest piece of the consecrated host.

I was very content to be a part of this celebration even though I was a little lightheaded during the consecration. When it was my turn to receive the Blessed Sacrament, Father broke off a small piece for me and recited the words, "The body of Christ." "Amen," I replied as he placed the tiny fragment of host in my hand. It was so small that I could hardly see it without my glasses (another frustration of middle age). I gazed at this white speck and was filled with a sense of awe and wonder. Yes, even this minute crumb of bread truly was the body of Christ. I replied, "Amen," received the precious body of our Lord in my mouth, and returned to my seat filled with the knowledge that all things are possible with God. My senses were keenly aware that there was no other sustenance in my body; it was Christ alone that sustained me. My physical emptiness had been replaced with Christ's spiritual nourishment and a heightened intimacy with God. He alone fills me. He completes me. It is the gift of his body alone that saves me; on Christ my life depends.

This event remains with me and continues to nourish me when I am feeling a little despondent about growing older. Age does have its blessings. With age comes wisdom, although I am not sure if my gratitude and love for the Eucharist are signs of wisdom or an effect of grace. I only know that I recognize more deeply and humbly the gift Jesus shares with my aging body in the Eucharist—everlasting life. Amen.

Even in Famine We Are Fed

Anonymous

We all know the story of Pharoah's dream of seven fat cattle that were devoured by seven lean cattle. Joseph interpreted the dream as a sign that seven years of bounty would be followed by seven years of famine. Pharoah followed Joseph's advice to put aside a fifth of the grain produced during the plentiful years so that there would be enough food when the famine came (Genesis 41:25-36).

For a long time our family felt the joy of our "fat years." But four years ago things changed. My husband received radiation for prostate cancer. Our daughter's struggle with bipolar disease climaxed in her attempted suicide and the loss of custody of her two young children. I faced surgery for breast cancer. My faith felt shredded.

The only thing that kept me from despair was the store of spiritual nourishment that Christ has left us in the Eucharist. The Bread of Life continued to sustain me even as I felt so weak. In the midst of doubts and questioning and pain, there is still the taste of Jesus really with us in the food he stored and still shares with us at every Mass.

Even in famine we are fed.

Strength for Life's Trials

by Gloria V. Adams

The Lord often gives people an opportunity to share their testimony. I will share mine in the hope that it might encourage someone to receive the Eucharist as often as they can.

I was raised in the Methodist faith and converted to Catholicism in 1965 along with my five young children. We attended Mass regularly and participated in all the sacraments. I joined the Blessed Mother's Sodality and later served as prefect for three years.

My children joined the CYO, and the boys won several basketball trophies for the church team. We prayed for my husband to join the church, as well. He was baptized into the Catholic faith in 1970 and joined the Holy Name Society shortly after.

In 1974 my oldest son was a tragic victim of an attempted robbery, which took his life and left his two small children without a father. I was overcome by sadness, feelings of emptiness, and stress. I missed him so much. One Sunday after Mass, I was thinking about my son when I realized that even when you serve the Lord, you will sometimes have trials. I began to ask the Lord to help me overcome these feelings of grief. I thank God, because I know that he led me out of the darkness that had been bottled up inside me for almost two years.

In 1981 I became one of the first Eucharistic ministers installed at St. Edward's Church, under the training of Fr. Philip Linden. I received the precious body and blood of Jesus as often as I could and visualized myself seated at the table with Jesus and the apostles at the Last Supper. Knowing that I was united with Jesus through the Eucharist gave me the strength that I needed to face everyday problems. And when you are raising children, sometimes the problems can be many.

On October 1, 1993, my youngest child died of leukemia. I was his caregiver at the same time that I was caring for my husband, who died in 1998 after a nine-year battle with Alzheimer's disease. One of the many lessons that I learned over the years is that letting go is something we all have to go through, and that saying good-bye is part of every transition. I now realize that it was my regular reception of the Eucharist that gave me the strength to endure. I know that my Savior will always be with me, even when my loved ones will not.

I have learned from my experiences that you should strive to receive the precious body and blood of the Savior through the Eucharist as often as you can. It will strengthen your faith, assist you with today's trials, and help you to face your tomorrows.

A Sense of Peace

by Jane Gentry

A very tranquil feeling comes upon me when I receive the body and blood of our Lord—a sense of peacefulness, and more important, a time to meet with the Lord to talk things over.

Approximately four years ago, I was diagnosed with a

chronic joint disease and had extreme pain in my joints and nerve endings. It was during that time that I truly experienced the compassion of our Lord. He gave me the strength and fortitude I needed to get through that very difficult time.

I would feel emptiness without receiving the Eucharist at least once a week, since it has helped me greatly to overcome my disease and live a relatively normal life again. After receiving the Eucharist I can truly feel close to the Lord and know that he hears me when I ask for his blessings and healing. To feel this close to the Lord is truly an extraordinary experience and a precious gift that I will cherish all my life.

Questions for Reflection

1. Think back to a trying situation in your life. How did you gain the strength each day to face your situation? How did your faith in God and in Jesus' presence in the Eucharist help you? Where else did you find strength and support?

2. Jesus said, "Come to me, all who labor and are heavy laden, and I will give you rest" (Matthew 11:28). When you are feeling weary and burdened, is your first impulse to come to Jesus in the Eucharist? Why or why not?

3. Why do you think we are often tempted to depend on ourselves for strength rather than on the Lord? If this is a temptation for you, what can you do to combat it?

CHAPTER 9

How to Write and Share Your Own Personal Witness

by TJSonni

Once we have truly met the Risen
One by partaking of his body and
blood, we cannot keep to ourselves
the joy we have experienced. . . . For
the Eucharist is a mode of being,
which passes from Jesus into each
Christian, through whose testimony
it is meant to spread throughout
society and culture.

—Pope John Paul II

D o you have a story of faith to share with others? Many of us think that if we haven't experienced a dramatic conversion, we won't have anything to share that would inspire others to draw closer to the Lord. That's probably not true. When we think back over our lives for instances in which the Lord has touched us, there is probably more than one story that will touch others as well. Many of the stories in this book did not involve dramatic circumstances, but they all illustrate, in concrete terms, that God is alive today and present in the Eucharist and in his body, the church.

As Catholics, we don't often see ourselves as evangelizers. We can be turned off by the idea of "Bible thumping" or "pushing" our religion onto others. We might even worry about sounding prideful.

However, sharing our faith and helping it to grow in the hearts of others is central to the purpose of a mature Christian life. While our spirituality has a very personal dimension, it is not private, because we are part of a larger community of believers. Our spiritual life cannot be self-centered. It must be self-giving by nature, since that is God's nature. When we share our story humbly and from the heart, those we speak with are likely to be touched and inspired to seek that same connection to the Lord. Taking the time to write out our witness, as the contributors of the stories in this book have done, will prepare us for those opportunities to share what the Lord has done in our lives.

There is one simple rule to consider when writing and sharing your witness: the rule of love. Anything else falls short of God's blessing. Make love your reason for beginning and your goal at the end. "Love the Lord your God with all your heart, and with all your soul, and with all your mind. . . . Love your neighbor as yourself." (Matthew 22:37-39). Let this twofold principle be your touchstone and your guide as you prepare to put your thoughts on paper.

Motivated by love for God and for others, particularly whoever will read or hear your witness, you need just one more thing to put you in the right frame of reference: an attitude of surrender. Let go of the result. It's natural for you to want to receive wonderful feedback from your witness. And it's only human to hope that your efforts to share your faith story will have a positive impact on others. Letting go of the outcome will make possible the sweet peace found in surrendering yourself to the Lord. That peace can add a spiritual magnetism to your writing and sharing, enabling God to speak through you. Such an attitude of selflessness opens you to God's grace. As a result, your witness will be a conduit of God's love, through which those who read or hear it are more likely to be drawn closer to him.

Writing Your Witness

Consider these steps in writing your witness, asking for the guidance and inspiration of the Holy Spirit at each step:

1. Think back over your faith life. In what ways has your faith made a difference? How has God touched you and others? After prayer and reflection, make a list of experiences and insights that you might want to include in your witness.

2. Begin to make the connections on your list and organize the elements that go together.

3. Find a starting point by going back to the earliest experience, and devise a natural beginning to your story.

4. Then create a first draft in which you share your experiences and feelings in straightforward and humble terms. All the glory belongs to the Lord, anyway.

5. When you have finished telling your story, look back at how you began. Often we learn more about our own faith in the process of writing about it. Does anything stand out that could sum up or tie together what you've written? Use those thoughts to conclude your witness.

6. After a few days, read through your first draft and edit it for clarity, direction, and emphasis.

7. Share your witness with a few people you know and love, asking for their candid overall feedback and for specific ways that it might be improved.

8. Finally, incorporate their feedback as it seems most appropriate, especially where there are common points shared by others.

Sharing Your Witness

Think about people you know who might appreciate hearing your witness. You can tell them how it came about as a part of this project, and ask them if they would be interested in reading it. Or you could just send it by e-mail to a group of people who you think might appreciate it. To spread the movement of faith sharing on the enormous blessing of the Eucharist, you might suggest that they consider writing their own testimony and sharing it with others. That is the ripple effect that we hope will be inspired by this book. If they are uncomfortable writing or sharing their own testimony, they could consider giving a copy of this book to someone they feel would be blessed by it. A short handwritten note could be added in the front of the book, and they could even point out some of their favorite testimonies or any that might seem particularly relevant to their friend.

As you think about sharing your own witness, remember that your only motivation is your love for God and others. Remember to "let go" in total surrender. Dare to share your love for the Lord in the Eucharist. Then let God do the rest. Your sharing may be only the planting of a seed that comes to harvest much later. Trust that the Lord will use your humble and loving efforts in some way for good. May you be the mighty blessing God wants you to be in the lives of others.

Apostolic Letter
Mane Nobiscum Domine

OF THE HOLY FATHER JOHN PAUL II

TO THE BISHOPS, CLERGY, AND FAITHFUL

FOR THE YEAR OF THE EUCHARIST

OCTOBER 2004—OCTOBER 2005

Introduction

1. "Stay with us, Lord, for it is almost evening" (cf. Luke 24:29). This was the insistent invitation that the two disciples journeying to Emmaus on the evening of the day of the resurrection addressed to the Wayfarer who had accompanied them on their journey. Weighed down with sadness, they never imagined that this stranger was none other than their Master, risen from the dead. Yet they felt their hearts burning within them (cf. v. 32) as he spoke to them and "explained" the Scriptures. The light of the Word unlocked the hardness of their hearts and "opened their eyes" (cf. v. 31). Amid the shadows of the passing day and the darkness that clouded their spirit, the Wayfarer brought a ray of light which rekindled their hope and led their hearts to yearn for the fullness of light. "Stay with us," they pleaded. And he agreed. Soon afterwards, Jesus' face would disappear, yet the Master would "stay" with them, hidden in the "breaking of the bread" which had opened their eyes to recognize him.

2. The *image of the disciples on the way to Emmaus* can serve as a fitting guide for a Year when the Church will be particularly engaged in living out the mystery of the Holy Eucharist. Amid our questions and difficulties, and even our bitter disappointments, the divine Wayfarer continues to walk at our side, opening to us the Scriptures and leading us to a deeper understanding of the mysteries of God. When we meet him fully, we will pass from the light of the Word to the light streaming from the "Bread of life," the supreme fulfillment of

his promise to "be with us always, to the end of the age" (cf. Matthew 28:20).

3. The "breaking of bread"—as the Eucharist was called in earliest times—has always been at the center of the Church's life. Through it Christ makes present within time the mystery of his death and resurrection. In it he is received in person as the "living bread come down from heaven" (John 6:51), and with him we receive the pledge of eternal life and a foretaste of the eternal banquet of the heavenly Jerusalem. Following the teaching of the Fathers, the Ecumenical Councils and my own Predecessors, I have frequently urged the Church to reflect upon the Eucharist, most recently in the *Encyclical Ecclesia de Eucharistia.* Here I do not intend to repeat this teaching, which I trust will be more deeply studied and understood. At the same time I thought it helpful for this purpose *to dedicate an entire Year to this wonderful sacrament.*

4. As is known, the *Year of the Eucharist* will be celebrated from October 2004 to October 2005. The idea for this celebration came from two events which will serve to mark its beginning and end: the *International Eucharistic Congress,* which will take place from 10 to 17 October 2004 in Guadalajara, Mexico, and the *Ordinary Assembly of the Synod of Bishops,* which will be held in the Vatican from 2 to 29 October 2005 on the theme: "The Eucharist: Source and Summit of the Life and Mission of the Church." I was also guided by another consideration: this year's *World Youth Day* will take place in Cologne from 16 to 21 August 2005. I would like the young people to gather around the Eucharist as the vital source which nourishes their faith and enthusiasm. A

Eucharistic initiative of this kind had been on my mind for some time: it is a natural development of the pastoral impulse which I wanted to give to the Church, particularly during the years of preparation for the Jubilee and in the years that followed it.

5. In the present Apostolic Letter, I wish to reaffirm this pastoral continuity and to help everyone to grasp its spiritual significance. As for the particular form which the Year of the Eucharist will take, I am counting on the personal involvement of the Pastors of the particular Churches, whose devotion to this great Mystery will not fail to suggest suitable approaches. My Brother Bishops will certainly understand that this initiative, coming as it does so soon after the celebration of the *Year of the Rosary,* is meant to take place on a deeply spiritual level, so that it will in no way interfere with the pastoral programs of the individual Churches. Rather, it can shed light upon those programs, anchoring them, so to speak, in the very Mystery which nourishes the spiritual life of the faithful and the initiatives of each local Church. I am not asking the individual Churches to alter their pastoral programs, but to emphasize the Eucharistic dimension which is part of the whole Christian life. For my part, I would like in this Letter to offer *some basic guidelines;* and I am confident that the People of God, at every level, will welcome my proposal with enthusiasm and fervent love.

I
In the Wake of the Council and the Great Jubilee

Looking towards Christ

6. Ten years ago, in *Tertio Millennio Adveniente* (10 November 1994), I had the joy of proposing to the Church a program of preparation for the *Great Jubilee of the Year 2000*. It seemed to me that this historic moment presented itself as a great grace. I realized, of course, that a simple chronological event, however evocative, could not by itself bring about great changes. Unfortunately the Millennium began with events which were in tragic continuity with the past, and often with its worst aspects. A scenario emerged which, despite certain positive elements, is marred by acts of violence and bloodshed which cause continued concern. Even so, in inviting the Church to celebrate the Jubilee of the two-thousandth anniversary of the Incarnation, I was convinced—and I still am, more than ever!—that this celebration would be of benefit to humanity in the "long term."

Jesus Christ stands at the center not just of the history of the Church, but also the history of humanity. In him, all things are drawn together (cf. Ephesians 1:10; Colossians 1:15-20). How could we forget the enthusiasm with which the Second Vatican Council, quoting Pope Paul VI, proclaimed that Christ is "the goal of human history, the focal point of the desires of history and civilization, the centre of mankind, the joy of all hearts, and the fulfillment of all aspirations"?[1] The Council's teaching gave added depth to our understanding of the nature of the Church, and gave believers a clearer insight not only into the mysteries of faith but also into earthly realities, seen in the light of Christ. In the Incarnate Word, both the mystery of God and the mystery of man are revealed.[2] In him, humanity finds redemption and fulfillment.

7. In the Encyclical *Redemptor Hominis*, at the beginning of my Pontificate, I developed this idea, and I have frequently returned to it on other occasions. The Jubilee was a fitting time to invite believers once again to consider this fundamental truth. The preparation for the great event was fully Trinitarian and Christocentric. Within this plan, there clearly had to be a place for the Eucharist. At the start of this Year of the Eucharist, I repeat the words which I wrote in *Tertio Millennio Adveniente*: "The Year 2000 will be intensely Eucharistic; in the *Sacrament of the Eucharist* the Savior, who took flesh in Mary's womb twenty centuries ago, continues to offer himself to humanity as the source of divine life."[3] The International Eucharistic Congress, held that year in Rome, also helped to focus attention on this aspect of the Great Jubilee. It is also worth recalling that my Apostolic Letter *Dies Domini*, written in preparation for the Jubilee, invited believers to meditate on Sunday as the day of the Risen Lord and the special day of the Church. At that time I urged everyone to rediscover the celebration of the Eucharist as the heart of Sunday.[4]

Contemplating with Mary the face of Christ

8. The fruits of the Great Jubilee were collected in the Apostolic Letter *Novo Millennio Ineunte*. In this programmatic document, I suggested an ever greater pastoral engagement based on the contemplation of the face of Christ, as part of an ecclesial pedagogy aimed at "the high standard" of holiness and carried out especially through the art of prayer.[5] How could such a program be complete without a commitment to the liturgy and in particular to the *cultivation of Eucharistic life?* As I said at the time: "In the twentieth century, especially since the Council, there has been a great development in the way the Christian community celebrates the Sacraments, especially the Eucharist. It is necessary to continue in this direction, and to stress particularly *the Sunday Eucharist* and *Sunday* itself, experienced as a special day of faith, the day of the Risen Lord and of the gift of the Spirit, the true weekly Easter."[6] In this context of a training in prayer, I recommended the celebration of the *Liturgy of the Hours,* by which the Church sanctifies the different hours of the day and the passage of time through the liturgical year.

9. Subsequently, with the proclamation of the Year of the Rosary and the publication of the Apostolic Letter *Rosarium Virginis Mariae*, I returned to the theme of contemplating the face of Christ, now from a Marian perspective, by encouraging once more the recitation of the Rosary. This traditional prayer, so highly recommended by the Magisterium and so dear to the People of God, has a markedly biblical and evangelical character, focused on the name and the face of Jesus as contemplated

in the mysteries and by the repetition of the "Hail Mary." In its flow of repetitions, it represents *a kind of pedagogy of love,* aimed at evoking within our hearts the same love that Mary bore for her Son. For this reason, developing a centuries-old tradition by the addition of the mysteries of light, I sought to make this privileged form of contemplation an even more complete "compendium of the Gospel."[7] And how could the mysteries of light not culminate in the Holy Eucharist?

From the Year of the Rosary to the Year of the Eucharist

10. In the midst of the *Year of the Rosary,* I issued the Encyclical Letter *Ecclesia de Eucharistia,* with the intention of shedding light on the mystery of the Eucharist in its inseparable and vital relation to the Church. I urged all the faithful to celebrate the Eucharistic sacrifice with due reverence, offering to Jesus present in the Eucharist, both within and outside Mass, the worship demanded by so great a Mystery. Above all, I suggested once again the need for a Eucharistic spirituality and pointed to Mary, "woman of the Eucharist,"[8] as its model.

The *Year of the Eucharist* takes place against *a background which has been enriched by the passage of the years,* while remaining ever rooted in the theme of Christ and the contemplation of his face. In a certain sense, it is meant to be a year of synthesis, *the high-point of a journey in progress.* Much could be said about how to celebrate this year. I would simply offer some reflections intended to help us all to experience it in a deeper and more fruitful way.

II
The Eucharist: a Mystery of Light

"He interpreted to them in all the Scriptures the things concerning himself" (Luke 24:27)

11. The account of the Risen Jesus appearing to the two disciples on the road to Emmaus helps us to focus on a primary aspect of the Eucharistic mystery, one which should always be present in the devotion of the People of God: *The Eucharist is a mystery of light!* What does this mean, and what are its implications for Christian life and spirituality?

Jesus described himself as the "light of the world" (John 8:12), and this quality clearly appears at those moments in his life, like the Transfiguration and the Resurrection, in which his divine glory shines forth brightly. Yet in the Eucharist the glory of Christ remains veiled. The Eucharist is pre-eminently a *mysterium fidei*. Through the mystery of his complete hiddenness, Christ becomes a mystery of light, thanks to which believers are led into the depths of the divine life. By a happy intuition, Rublëv's celebrated icon of the Trinity clearly places the Eucharist at the center of the life of the Trinity.

12. The Eucharist is light above all because at every Mass the liturgy of the Word of God precedes the liturgy of the Eucharist in the unity of the two "tables," the table of the Word and the table of the Bread. This continuity is expressed in the Eucharistic discourse of Saint John's Gospel, where Jesus begins his teaching by speaking of the mystery of his person and then goes on to draw out its Eucharistic dimension: "My

flesh is food indeed, and my blood is drink indeed" (John 6:55). We know that this was troubling for most of his listeners, which led Peter to express the faith of the other Apostles and of the Church throughout history: "Lord, to whom can we go? You have the words of eternal life" (John 6:68). In the account of the disciples on the road to Emmaus, Christ himself intervenes to show, "beginning with Moses and all the prophets," how "all the Scriptures" point to the mystery of his person (cf. Luke 24:27). His words make the hearts of the disciples "burn" within them, drawing them out of the darkness of sorrow and despair, and awakening in them a desire to remain with him: "Stay with us, Lord" (cf. v. 29).

13. The Fathers of the Second Vatican Council, in the Constitution *Sacrosanctum Concilium*, sought to make "the table of the word" offer the treasures of Scripture more fully to the faithful.[9] Consequently they allowed the biblical readings of the liturgy to be proclaimed in a language understood by all. It is Christ himself who speaks when the Holy Scriptures are read in the Church.[10] The Council Fathers also urged the celebrant to treat the homily as part of the liturgy, aimed at explaining the word of God and drawing out its meaning for the Christian life.[11] Forty years after the Council, the *Year of the Eucharist* can serve as an important opportunity for Christian communities *to evaluate their progress in this area.* It is not enough that the biblical passages are read in the vernacular, if they are not also proclaimed with the care, preparation, devout attention and meditative silence that enable the word of God to touch people's minds and hearts.

"They recognized him in the breaking of bread" *(cf. Luke 24:35)*

14. It is significant that the two disciples on the road to Emmaus, duly prepared by our Lord's words, recognized him at table through the simple gesture of the "breaking of bread." When minds are enlightened and hearts are enkindled, signs begin to "speak." The Eucharist unfolds in a dynamic context of signs containing a rich and luminous message. Through these signs the mystery in some way opens up before the eyes of the believer.

As I emphasized in my Encyclical *Ecclesia de Eucharistia*, it is important that no dimension of this sacrament should be neglected. We are constantly tempted to reduce the Eucharist to our own dimensions, while in reality *it is we who must open ourselves up to the dimensions of the Mystery.* "The Eucharist is too great a gift to tolerate ambiguity and depreciation."[12]

15. There is no doubt that the most evident dimension of the Eucharist is that it is a *meal*. The Eucharist was born, on the evening of Holy Thursday, in the setting of the Passover meal. *Being a meal* is part of its very structure. "Take, eat . . . Then he took a cup and . . . gave it to them, saying: Drink from it, all of you" (Matthew 26:26, 27). As such, it expresses the fellowship which God wishes to establish with us and which we ourselves must build with one another.

Yet it must not be forgotten that the Eucharistic meal also has a profoundly and primarily *sacrificial* meaning.[13] In the Eucharist, Christ makes present to us anew *the sacrifice offered once for all on Golgotha.* Present in the Eucharist as the Risen

Lord, he nonetheless bears the marks of his passion, of which every Mass is a "memorial," as the Liturgy reminds us in the acclamation following the consecration: "We announce your death, Lord, we proclaim your resurrection. . . ." At the same time, while the Eucharist makes present what occurred in the past, it also *impels us towards the future, when Christ will come again* at the end of history. This "eschatological" aspect makes the Sacrament of the Eucharist an event which draws us into itself and fills our Christian journey with hope.

"I am with you always . . ." (Matthew 28:20)

16. All these dimensions of the Eucharist come together in one aspect which more than any other makes a demand on our faith: *the mystery of the "real" presence.* With the entire tradition of the Church, we believe that Jesus is truly present under the Eucharistic species. This presence—as Pope Paul VI rightly explained—is called "real" not in an exclusive way, as if to suggest that other forms of Christ's presence are not real, but *par excellence,* because Christ thereby becomes substantially present, whole and entire, in the reality of his body and blood.[14] Faith demands that we approach the Eucharist fully aware that we are approaching Christ himself. It is precisely his presence which gives the other aspects of the Eucharist—as meal, as memorial of the Paschal Mystery, as eschatological anticipation—a significance which goes far beyond mere symbolism. The Eucharist is a mystery of presence, the perfect fulfillment of Jesus' promise to remain with us until the end of the world.

Celebrating, worshiping, contemplating

17. The Eucharist is a great mystery! And it is one which above all must be *well celebrated*. Holy Mass needs to be set at the center of the Christian life and celebrated in a dignified manner by every community, in accordance with established norms, with the participation of the assembly, with the presence of ministers who carry out their assigned tasks, and with a serious concern that singing and *liturgical music* be suitably "sacred." One specific project of this *Year of the Eucharist* might be for each parish community to study the General Instruction of the Roman Missal. The best way to enter into the mystery of salvation made present in the sacred "signs" remains that of following faithfully the unfolding of the liturgical year. Pastors should be committed to that *"mystagogical" catechesis* so dear to the Fathers of the Church, by which the faithful are helped to understand the meaning of the liturgy's words and actions, to pass from its signs to the mystery which they contain, and to enter into that mystery in every aspect of their lives.

18. There is a particular need to cultivate *a lively awareness of Christ's real presence,* both in the celebration of Mass and in the worship of the Eucharist outside Mass. Care should be taken to show that awareness through tone of voice, gestures, posture and bearing. In this regard, liturgical law recalls— and I myself have recently reaffirmed[15]—the importance of moments of silence both in the celebration of Mass and in Eucharistic adoration. The way that the ministers and the faithful treat the Eucharist should be marked by profound

respect.[16] The presence of Jesus in the tabernacle must be a kind of *magnetic pole* attracting an ever greater number of souls enamored of him, ready to wait patiently to hear his voice and, as it were, to sense the beating of his heart. "O taste and see that the Lord is good!" (Psalm 34:8).

During this year *Eucharistic adoration outside Mass* should become a particular commitment for individual parish and religious communities. Let us take the time to kneel before Jesus present in the Eucharist, in order to make reparation by our faith and love for the acts of carelessness and neglect, and even the insults which our Saviour must endure in many parts of the world. Let us deepen through adoration our personal and communal contemplation, drawing upon aids to prayer inspired by the word of God and the experience of so many mystics, old and new. The Rosary itself, when it is profoundly understood in the biblical and Christocentric form which I recommended in the Apostolic Letter *Rosarium Virginis Mariae,* will prove a particularly fitting introduction to Eucharistic contemplation, a contemplation carried out with Mary as our companion and guide.[17]

This year let us also celebrate with particular devotion the Solemnity of *Corpus Christi,* with its traditional procession. Our faith in the God who took flesh in order to become our companion along the way needs to be everywhere proclaimed, especially in our streets and homes, as an expression of our grateful love and as an inexhaustible source of blessings.

III
The Eucharist:
Source and Manifestation of Communion

"Abide in me, and I in you" (John 15:4)

19. When the disciples on the way to Emmaus asked Jesus to stay "with" them, he responded by giving them a much greater gift: through the Sacrament of the Eucharist he found a way to stay "in" them. Receiving the Eucharist means entering into a profound communion with Jesus. "Abide in me, and I in you" (John 15:4). This relationship of profound and mutual "abiding" *enables us to have a certain foretaste of heaven on earth.* Is this not the greatest of human yearnings? Is this not what God had in mind when he brought about in history his plan of salvation? God has placed in human hearts a "hunger" for his word (cf. Amos 8:11), a hunger which will be satisfied only by full union with him. Eucharistic communion was given so that we might be "sated" with God here on earth, in expectation of our complete fulfillment in heaven.

One bread, one body

20. This special closeness which comes about in Eucharistic "communion" cannot be adequately understood or fully experienced apart from ecclesial communion. I emphasized this repeatedly in my Encyclical *Ecclesia de Eucharistia.* The Church is the Body of Christ: we walk "with Christ" to the extent that we are in relationship "with his body." Christ pro-

vided for the creation and growth of this unity by the outpouring of his Holy Spirit. And he himself constantly builds it up by his Eucharistic presence. It is the one Eucharistic bread which makes us one body. As the Apostle Paul states: "Because there is one bread, we who are many are one body, for we all partake of the one bread" (1 Corinthians 10:17). In the mystery of the Eucharist Jesus builds up the Church as a communion, in accordance with the supreme model evoked in his *priestly prayer:* "Even as you, Father, are in me, and I in you, that they may also be in us, so that the world may believe that you have sent me" (John 17:21).

21. The Eucharist is both the *source* of ecclesial unity and its greatest *manifestation*. The Eucharist is an *epiphany of communion*. For this reason the Church sets conditions for full participation in the celebration of the Eucharist.[18] These various limitations ought to make us ever more conscious of *the demands made by the communion which Jesus asks of us*. It is a *hierarchical* communion, based on the awareness of a variety of roles and ministries, as is seen by the reference to the Pope and the Diocesan Bishop in the Eucharistic Prayer. It is a *fraternal* communion, cultivated by a "spirituality of communion" which fosters reciprocal openness, affection, understanding and forgiveness.[19]

". . . of one heart and soul" (Acts 4:32)

22. At each Holy Mass we are called to measure ourselves against the ideal of communion which the *Acts of the Apostles* paints as a model for the Church in every age. It is the Church

gathered around the Apostles, called by the word of God, capable of sharing in spiritual goods but in material goods as well (cf. Acts 2:42-47; 4:32-35). In this *Year of the Eucharist* the Lord invites us to draw as closely as possible to this ideal. Every effort should be made to experience fully those occasions mentioned in the liturgy for the Bishop's "Stational Mass," which he celebrates in the cathedral together with his presbyters and deacons, with the participation of the whole People of God. Here we see the principal "manifestation" of the Church.[20] It would be praiseworthy to specify *other significant occasions,* also on the parochial level, which would increase a sense of communion and find in the Eucharistic celebration a source of renewed fervor.

The Lord's Day

23. In a particular way I ask that every effort be made this year to experience Sunday as the day of the Lord and the day of the Church. I would be happy if everyone would reflect once more on my words in the Apostolic Letter *Dies Domini.* "At Sunday Mass, Christians relive with particular intensity the experience of the Apostles on the evening of Easter, when the Risen Lord appeared to them as they were gathered together (cf. John 20:19). In a sense, the People of God of all times were present in that small nucleus of disciples, the first-fruits of the Church."[21] During this year of grace, priests in their pastoral ministry should *be even more attentive to Sunday Mass* as the celebration which brings together the entire parish community, with the participation of different groups, movements and associations.

IV
The Eucharist:
Principle and Plan of "Mission"

"They set out immediately" (cf. Luke 24:33)

24. The two disciples of Emmaus, upon recognizing the Lord, "set out immediately" (cf. Luke 24:33), in order to report what they had seen and heard. Once we have truly met the Risen One by partaking of his body and blood, we cannot keep to ourselves the joy we have experienced. The encounter with Christ, constantly intensified and deepened in the Eucharist, issues in the Church and in every Christian *an urgent summons to testimony and evangelization.* I wished to emphasize this in my homily announcing the *Year of the Eucharist,* based on the words of Saint Paul: "As often as you eat this bread and drink the cup, you proclaim the Lord's death until he comes" (1 Corinthians 11:26). The Apostle closely relates meal and proclamation: entering into communion with Christ in the memorial of his Pasch also means sensing the duty to be a missionary of the event made present in that rite.[22] The dismissal at the end of each Mass is *a charge* given to Christians, inviting them to work for the spread of the Gospel and the imbuing of society with Christian values.

25. The Eucharist not only provides the interior strength needed for this mission, but is also—in some sense—*its plan.* For the Eucharist is a mode of being, which passes from Jesus into each Christian, through whose testimony it is meant to spread throughout society and culture. For this to happen,

each member of the faithful must assimilate, through personal and communal meditation, the values which the Eucharist expresses, the attitudes it inspires, the resolutions to which it gives rise. Can we not see here *a special charge* which could emerge from this *Year of the Eucharist?*

Giving thanks

26. One fundamental element of this *plan* is found in the very meaning of the word "Eucharist": thanksgiving. In Jesus, in his sacrifice, in his unconditional "yes" to the will of the Father, is contained the "yes," the "thank you" and the "amen" of all humanity. The Church is called to remind men and women of this great truth. This is especially urgent in the context of our secularized culture, characterized as it is by a forgetfulness of God and a vain pursuit of human self-sufficiency. Incarnating the Eucharistic "plan" in daily life, wherever people live and work—in families, schools, the workplace, in all of life's settings—means bearing witness that *human reality cannot be justified without reference to the Creator:* "Without the Creator the creature would disappear."[23] This transcendent point of reference, which commits us constantly to give thanks for all that we have and are—in other words, to a "Eucharistic" attitude—in no way detracts from the legitimate autonomy of earthly realities,[24] but grounds that autonomy more firmly by setting it within its proper limits.

In this *Year of the Eucharist* Christians ought to be committed to bearing more forceful witness to God's presence in the world. We should not be afraid to speak about God and to bear proud witness to our faith. The "culture of the Eucharist" promotes a culture of dialogue, which here finds strength and nourishment. It is a mistake to think that any public reference to faith will somehow undermine the rightful autonomy of the State and civil institutions, or that it can even encourage attitudes of intolerance. If history demonstrates that mistakes have also been made in this area by believers, as I acknowledged on the occasion of the Jubilee, this must be attributed not to "Christian roots," but to the failure of Christians to be faithful to those roots. One who learns to say "thank you" in the manner of the crucified Christ might end up as a martyr, but never as a persecutor.

The way of solidarity

27. The Eucharist is not merely an expression of communion in the Church's life; it is also a *project of solidarity* for all of humanity. In the celebration of the Eucharist the Church constantly renews her awareness of being a "sign and instrument" not only of intimate union with God but also of the unity of the whole human race.[25] Each Mass, even when celebrated in obscurity or in isolation, always has a universal character. The Christian who takes part in the Eucharist learns to become a *promoter of communion, peace and solidarity* in every situation. More than ever, our troubled world, which began the new Millennium with the specter of terrorism and the tragedy of war, demands that Christians learn to experience the Eucharist as a *great school of peace*, forming men and women who, at

various levels of responsibility in social, cultural and political life, can become promoters of dialogue and communion.

At the service of the least

28. There is one other point which I would like to emphasize, since it significantly affects the authenticity of our communal sharing in the Eucharist. It is the impulse which the Eucharist gives to the community for *a practical commitment to building a more just and fraternal society*. In the Eucharist our God has shown love in the extreme, overturning all those criteria of power which too often govern human relations and radically affirming the criterion of service: "If anyone would be first, he must be last of all and servant of all" (Mark 9:35). It is not by chance that the Gospel of John contains no account of the institution of the Eucharist, but instead relates the "washing of feet" (cf. John 13:1-20): by bending down to wash the feet of his disciples, Jesus explains the meaning of the Eucharist unequivocally. Saint Paul vigorously reaffirms the impropriety of a Eucharistic celebration lacking charity expressed by practical sharing with the poor (cf. 1 Corinthians 11:17-22, 27-34).

Can we not make this *Year of the Eucharist* an occasion for diocesan and parish communities to commit themselves in a particular way to responding with fraternal solicitude to one of the many forms of poverty present in our world? I think for example of the tragedy of hunger which plagues hundreds of millions of human beings, the diseases which afflict developing countries, the loneliness of the elderly, the hardships faced by the unemployed, the struggles of immigrants. These are evils which are present—albeit to a different degree—even in areas of immense wealth. We cannot delude ourselves: by our mutual love and, in particular, by our concern for those in need we will be recognized as true followers of Christ (cf. John 13:35; Matthew 25:31-46). This will be the criterion by which the authenticity of our Eucharistic celebrations is judged.

Conclusion

29. *O Sacrum Convivium, in quo Christus sumitur!* The *Year of the Eucharist* has its source in the amazement with which the Church contemplates this great Mystery. It is an amazement which I myself constantly experience. It prompted my Encyclical *Ecclesia de Eucharistia*. As I look forward to the twenty-seventh year of my Petrine ministry, I consider it a great grace to be able to call the whole Church to contemplate, praise, and adore in a special way this ineffable Sacrament. May the *Year of the Eucharist* be for everyone a precious opportunity to grow in awareness of the incomparable treasure which Christ has entrusted to his Church. May it encourage a more lively and fervent celebration of the Eucharist, leading to a Christian life transformed by love.

There is room here for any number of initiatives, according to the judgment of the Pastors of the particular Churches. The *Congregation for Divine Worship and the Discipline of the Sacraments* will not fail to provide some helpful suggestions and proposals. I do not ask, however, for anything extraordinary, but rather that every initiative be marked by a profound interiority. If the only result of this Year were the revival in all Christian communities of the celebration of Sunday Mass and an increase in Eucharistic worship outside Mass, this Year of grace would be abundantly successful. At the same time, it is good to aim high, and not to be content with mediocrity, since we know we can always count on God's help.

30. To you, dear *Brother Bishops,* I commend this Year, confident that you will welcome my invitation with full apostolic zeal.

Dear *priests,* who repeat the words of consecration each day, and are witnesses and heralds of the great miracle of love which takes place at your hands: be challenged by the grace of this special Year; celebrate Holy Mass each day with the same joy and fervor with which you celebrated your first Mass, and willingly spend time in prayer before the tabernacle.

May this be a Year of grace also for you, *deacons,* who are so closely engaged in the ministry of the word and the service of the altar. I ask you, *lectors, acolytes and extraordinary ministers of holy communion,* to become ever more aware of the gift you have received in the service entrusted to you for a more worthy celebration of the Eucharist.

In particular I appeal to you, *the priests of the future.* During your time in the seminary make every effort to experience the beauty not only of taking part daily in Holy Mass, but also of spending a certain amount of time in dialogue with the Eucharistic Lord.

Consecrated men and women, called by that very consecration to more prolonged contemplation: never forget that Jesus in the tabernacle wants you to be at his side, so that he can fill your hearts with the experience of his friendship, which alone gives meaning and fulfillment to your lives.

May all of you, *the Christian faithful,* rediscover the gift of the Eucharist as light and strength for your daily lives in the world, in the exercise of your respective professions amid so many different situations. Rediscover this above all in order to experience fully the beauty and the mission of the *family.*

I have great expectations of you, *young people,* as I look forward to our meeting at the next *World Youth Day* in Cologne. The theme of our meeting—"*We have come to worship him*"—suggests how you can best experience this Eucharistic year. Bring to your encounter with Jesus, hidden in the Eucharist, all the enthusiasm of your age, all your hopes, all your desire to love.

31. We have before us the example of the Saints, who in the Eucharist found nourishment on their journey towards perfection. How many times did they shed tears of profound emotion in the presence of this great mystery, or experience hours of inexpressible "spousal" joy before the sacrament of the altar! May we be helped above all by the Blessed Virgin Mary, whose whole life incarnated the meaning of the Eucharist. "The Church, which looks to Mary as a model, is also called to imitate her in her relationship with this most holy mystery."[26] The Eucharistic Bread which we receive is the spotless flesh of her Son: *Ave verum corpus natum de Maria Virgine.* In this Year of grace, sustained by Mary, may the

Church discover new enthusiasm for her mission and come to acknowledge ever more fully that the Eucharist is the source and summit of her entire life.

To all of you I impart my Blessing as a pledge of grace and joy.

From the Vatican, on 7 October, the Memorial of Our Lady of the Rosary, in the year 2004, the twenty-sixth of my Pontificate.

Ioannes Paulus PP.II

Notes

[1] Pastoral Constitution on the Church in the Modern World *Gaudium et Spes*, 45.

[2] Cf. *ibid.*, 22.

[3] No. 55: *AAS* 87 (1995), 38.

[4] Cf. Nos. 32-34: *AAS* 90 (1998), 732-734.

[5] Cf. Nos. 30-32: *AAS* 93 (2001), 287-289.

[6] *Ibid.*, 35: *loc. cit.*, 290-291.

[7] Cf. Apostolic Letter *Rosarium Virginis Mariae* (16 October 2002), 19-21: *AAS* 95 (2003), 18-20.

[8] Encyclical Letter *Ecclesia de Eucharistia* (17 April 2003), 53: *AAS* 95 (2003), 469.

[9] Cf. No. 51.

[10] *Ibid.*, 7.

[11] Cf *ibid.*, 52.

[12]Encyclical Letter *Ecclesia de Eucharistia* (17 April 2003), 10: *AAS* 95 (2003), 439.

[13]Cf. John Paul II, Encyclical Letter *Ecclesia de Eucharistia* (17 April 2003), 10: *AAS* 95 (2003), 439. Congregation for Divine Worship and the Discipline of the Sacraments, Instruction *Redemptionis Sacramentum* on certain matters to be observed or to be avoided regarding the Most Holy Eucharist (25 March 2004), 38: *L'Osservatore Romano,* Weekly Edition in English, 28 April 2004, Special Insert, p.3.

[14]Cf. Encyclical Letter *Mysterium Fidei* (3 September 1965), 39: *AAS* 57 (1965), 764; Sacred Congregation of Rites, Instruction *Eucharisticum Mysterium* on the Worship of the Eucharistic Mystery (25 May 1967), 9: *AAS* 59 (1967), 547.

[15]Cf. Message *Spiritus et Sponsa,* for the fortieth anniversary of the Constitution on the Sacred Liturgy *Sacrosanctum Concilium* (4 December 2003), 13: *AAS* 96 (2004), 425.

[16]Cf. Congregation for Divine Worship and the Discipline of the Sacraments, Instruction *Redemptionis Sacramentum* on certain matters to be observed or to be avoided regarding the Most Holy Eucharist (25 March 2004): *L'Osservatore Romano,* Weekly Edition in English, 28 April 2004, Special Insert.

[17]Cf. *ibid.,* 137, *loc. cit.,* p.11.

[18]Cf. John Paul II, Encyclical Letter *Ecclesia de Eucharistia* (17 April 2003), 44: *AAS* 95 (2003), 462; *Code of Canon Law,* canon 908; *Code of Canons of the Eastern Churches,* canon 702; Pontifical Council for Promoting Christian Unity, *Directorium Oecumenicum* (25 March 1993), 122-125, 129-131: *AAS* 85 (1993), 1086-1089; Congregation for the Doc-

trine of the Faith, Letter *A.d. Exsequendam* (18 May 2001): *AAS* 93 (2001), 786.

[19]Cf. John Paul II, Apostolic Letter *Novo Millennio Ineunte* (6 January 2001), 43: *AAS* 93 (2001), 297.

[20]Cf. Second Vatican Ecumenical Council, Constitution on the Sacred Liturgy *Sacrosanctum Concilium*, 41.

[21]No. 33: *AAS* 90 (1998), 733.

[22]Cf. Homily for the Solemnity of the Body and Blood of Christ (10 June 2004): *L'Osservatore Romano*, 11-12 June 2004, p.6.

[23]Second Vatican Ecumenical Council, Pastoral Constitution on the Church in the Modern World *Gaudium et Spes*, 36.

[24]*Ibid.*

[25]Cf. Second Vatican Ecumenical Council, Pastoral Constitution on the Church *Lumen Gentium*, 1.

[26]John Paul II, Encyclical Letter *Ecclesia de Eucharistia* (17 April 2003), 53: *AAS* 95 (2003), 469.